DO YOU SEE WHAT I'M SAYING?

WALKING BY FAITH; TRUSTING GOD'S GUIDANCE EVERY STEP OF THE WAY

DR. SHAWN M. NICHOLSON

DR. SHAWN M. NICHOLSON

Do You See What I'm Saying? Walking By Faith; Trusting God's Guidance Every Step of the Way.

Copyright ©2023 by L3 Publishing House,
"Unleashing the Power of Words, One Word at a Time"

All rights reserved. No part of this book may be reproduced or transmitted in any form or by any means without written permission from the author.

ISBN: 978-0-578-35519-1

eBook ISBN: 9781088172476

Author photograph by Paris Lovette Vette Photography
https://www.vettephotography.com

Cover layout and design by: Odaro Samuel Osakpolor

For booking contact:
booking@drshawnmnicholson.com
www.drshawnmnicholson.com

DEDICATION

This book is dedicated to all the dreamers, the seekers, and the courageous souls who understand that there is more to life than what meets the eye. It is for those who believe in the God of possibility, the strength of resilience, and the beauty of embracing the unknown.

To those who dare to believe in the invisible, to those who trust in the power of words, and to those who choose to walk by faith in a world of uncertainty. Do You See What I'm Saying? Walking By Faith: Trusting God's Guidance Every Step of the Way.

To my family, whose unwavering support and love have carried me through every step of this journey. Your belief in me has been my anchor, and I am eternally grateful and value the legacy of faith.

To my friends, who have been my pillars of strength, my sounding boards, and my biggest cheerleaders. Thank you for lending me your ears, your hearts, and your encouragement and prayers.

To my mentors, coaches, and teachers, past and present who have imparted their wisdom and guided me towards the path of self-discovery. Your invaluable insights have help shaped my perspective and fueled my growth as a writer and as a servant of God.

To the readers, both old and new, who have embraced my words and allowed them to resonate within your souls. Your unwavering support and connection have given my words meaning and purpose. It is for you that I continue to write, hoping to touch hearts and ignite sparks of inspiration and activate your passion, potential, and purpose.

May this book serve as a reminder that even when the world seems chaotic, and the road ahead appears uncertain, there is a guiding light within us all. May it encourage you to see beyond the obvious, to trust in the whispers of your intuition, and to walk by faith with unwavering determination,

DR. SHAWN M. NICHOLSON

DO YOU SEE WHAT I'M SAYING?

WALKING BY FAITH; TRUSTING GOD'S GUIDANCE EVERY STEP OF THE WAY

DO YOU SEE WHAT I'M SAYING

TABLE OF CONTENTS

INTRODUCTION 11

CHAPTER ONE 13
    Who we are 15
    We are Children of God 17
    We are New Creations in Christ 18
    We are Ambassadors of Christ 20
    We are Part of the Body of Christ 21
    We are called to Holiness 22
    Our Image in Christ 23
    We are Loved 24
    We are Forgiven 24
    We are Chosen 25
    We are Empowered 25
    We are Called to be like Him 25
    Our Identity in Christ 25
    Our Integrity 28

CHAPTER TWO 29
    Whose we are 31
    What it Means to Belong to God 32
    We Belong to God Because He Created Us 33
    We Belong to God Because We Are His Children 34
    We Belong to God Because He Redeemed Us 35
    We Belong to God Because He has a Purpose for Our Lives 36

CHAPTER THREE 36
    Why Are We Here? 37
    Why God Created Us 39
    Be fruitful and multiply 39
    To have Dominion 41
    To Replenish the World 42
    To Reconcile the World With God 43
    We Were Born to Serve 44
    To Value People 45

    To glorify God and to enjoy Him forever 45
CHAPTER FOUR 46
    Power vs Authority 47
    How to Use Power and Authority in a Godly Way.
    Develop a Servant's Heart 50
    Seek the wisdom and guidance of God 52
    Being humble and submitting to others 53
    Seeking justice and righteousness 55
CHAPTER FIVE 59
    Having Faith In God 59
    Why is Faith Important? 64
    How Can We Develop and Maintain Our Faith? 65
CHAPTER SIX 67
    Walking By Faith 67
    What Walking by Faith Is Not 70
    Walking by faith is not the same as being an enterprising businessman 70
    Walking by faith does not mean being lazy or failing to make plans 70
    Walking by faith does not mean walking according to your feelings 71
    Ways to Walk by Faith 71
    Surrender 71
    Refocus 72
    Standing on God's Promises 73

CHAPTER SEVEN 76
    Kingdom Business 76
    What Makes a Business a Kingdom Business? 76

DO YOU SEE WHAT I'M SAYING

A Christian or Christians With a Large or Small Sphere of Influence 77
A Mission That Goes Beyond and Goes Deeper Than Just Making Money 77
A product or service that fits with God's plan for the world 77
The Client Is Valued For Who They Are, Not Just For What They Can Bring In Financially 78
The business suggests the presence of the Kingdom and encourages the opportunity to witness 78
Workers and employees are provided with the tools necessary to realize their full potential in life 78
The Purpose of the Kingdom Aligned With the Culture of the Organization 79
The Leaders are Servants 79
Grace is the engine that drives the business 79
The Intersection of Ministry and Business 80
Pastoring Beyond the four walls 81

CHAPTER EIGHT 85
Speak the Word Only 86
How do we apply this principle of speaking the word only in our daily lives? 87
First confess with your mouth 88
Whatever God will deliver into your hand 89

CHAPTER NINE 93
Fishers of men 93
Types of fish 97
The Builders 97
The Baby Boomers 97
The Gen-Xers, Xennials, Millennials, and Gen-Alphas 98
Types of Baits 99
Personal testimony 99

Service and kindness	99
Prayer	99
Scripture	99
Relationships	99
Types of water	100
Calm waters	100
Rough waters	100
Deep waters	100
Shallow waters	101
Murky waters	101
CHAPTER TEN	103
Understanding God's timing	103
When Waiting on God Seems to Be Taking Forever	106
Patiently wait	107
Learn to Embrace God's Timing	108
Learn to Trust God	109
Conclusion	111
Affirmations	112
Prayers	113

PREFACE

Do you ever feel as if you are going through the motions of life without any particular purpose or direction in mind? Do you want to have a more intimate connection with God and a more profound understanding of the plan that he has for your life? The book "Do You See What I'm Saying? Walking By Faith: Trusting God's Guidance Every Step of the Way, focuses on the concept of faith and how it might influence our lives. At its core, faith is about trusting in God's love and wisdom even when we don't fully understand His ways. It is the foundation upon which our relationship with God is built, and it is through faith that we can experience His grace, mercy, and power in our lives.

This book answers the commonly asked questions like "Who are we? Whose are we?", "Why are we here"? and many other faith-based question bothering many Christians. It is a book that examines the details of our purpose and mission on earth. Are you looking to discovering your power and authority in Jesus Christ? If so, you can't afford to not have this book in your library because it emphasizes the importance of faith as a way of life and encourages readers to develop a more personal relationship with God. It provides a range of practical tips and strategies for cultivating a deeper faith, including guidance on prayer, Bible study, and other spiritual practices.

DR. SHAWN M. NICHOLSON

ABOUT THE AUTHOR:

Dr. Shawn M. Nicholson is an Author, Entrepreneur, Community Advocate, and a Servant Leader. He is also the founder and planter of Beautiful Temple Ministries, a community-rooted outreach church ministry centered on loving people to life. He has always believed in Kingdom Business and helping others see the intersection between ministry and business as well as teaching how to live an abundant, holistic life. Rapidly becoming a globally respected thought leader who is devoted to helping individuals activate their passion, potential, and purpose.

For the past 25 years, Dr. Nicholson has used the gifts God has given him to be an innovative, strategic leader with a passion for working in partnership with Black and Brown communities to eradicate generational poverty and stimulate economic prosperity for those who have been most excluded from it. Standing on the principals provided through scriptures to walk by faith.

Lastly, Dr. Nicholson is the author of two additional books,
PASS-I-ON® (7 Building Blocks to Sustainability and Success) and Teach Me How to Pivot (Planning, Innovating Vison, Outway, Threats).

INTRODUCTION

The author pulls from a variety of anecdotes and passages from the Bible all throughout the book to highlight the strength that comes from putting one's faith into action. For instance, he talks about how Abraham's trust in God allowed him to leave his country and move to a new place. It also talks about how Moses' confidence in God enabled him to lead the Israelites out of Egypt and how Noah prepared for the flooding even though it had never rained on earth before.

The book also provides practical guidance on how to apply these principles of faith in our daily lives. For instance, it explores how we can pray with faith, how we can overcome fear and doubt, and how we can trust in God's provision even when things don't seem to be going our way.

One of the key themes of "Do You See What I'm Saying? Walking by Faith" is the idea that faith requires trust and surrender. The author emphasizes the importance of relinquishing control and allowing God to guide our lives, even when the path ahead is uncertain or difficult.

The book also addresses common challenges that many people face in their faith journeys, such as doubt, fear, and spiritual dryness. The book offers practical advice and encouragement to help readers overcome these obstacles and develop a stronger, more resilient faith. They share stories of people who have overcome seemingly insurmountable challenges through their faith in God, and they offer insights and inspiration to help readers stay focused on God's promises and plans for their lives.

Overall, "Do You See What I'm Saying? Walking by Faith" is a book that offers a thoughtful and practical approach to developing a deeper relationship with God. Whether you are new to the Christian faith or seeking to renew and strengthen your spiritual journey, this book offers insights and encouragement to help you navigate the challenges and uncertainties of life with confidence and hope.

DR. SHAWN M. NICHOLSON

One of the key themes of the book is the idea that walking by faith allows us to experience God's presence and provision in our lives. By trusting in God's plan, we can find peace and purpose even amid difficult circumstances. The author uses real-life examples and biblical stories to illustrate the power of faith in action and to show how it can transform lives.

Ultimately, "Do You See What I'm Saying? Walking by Faith" is a book about hope and the transformative power of faith. It reminds us that we are not alone in our struggles, and that God is always with us, guiding and supporting us along the way. Through its pages, readers will be inspired to deepen their relationship with God and to trust in His plan for their lives, even when the path ahead seems uncertain.

CHAPTER ONE
WHO WE ARE

Do you know who you are? I'm not talking about who you are because of your parents, your background, or your upbringing, but I mean do you *really* know who you are in Christ? Most people know who they are in the natural realm as it relates to their family and upbringing, but when it comes to their true identity in Christ and what that entails, they don't have a clue.

Often, people have a hard time identifying with Jesus, because they relate to their physical, natural identities and the things they can perceive with their senses more than they do with Him. In addition, they equate their outward behavior with their identity and think that what they *do* is who they *are*.
However, when we accept Jesus as our Lord and personal Savior, we become one with Him. Knowing who we are in Christ is the catalyst for walking in the power of God and demonstrating that power to the world. The knowledge of who we are in Christ is so vital to our confidence as Christians, and it is the area in which Satan will consistently attack us. In fact, he attacked Jesus in the area of identity when He was fasting in the wilderness for forty days and forty nights. When Satan tried to question Jesus' identity in the wilderness, Jesus responded with the Word of God (Matthew 4:1-7).

For example, When Satan said, *"If thou be the Son of God, command that these stones be made bread."* Jesus answered, *"It is written, Man shall not live by bread alone, but by every word that proceedeth out of the mouth of God."* Once Satan realized Jesus didn't have an identity problem, he left Him alone. Likewise, when Satan comes to attack our identity in Christ, we must remind him of what is written, and he will leave us alone too.

As human beings, we often wonder, "Who we are." This is a question that has been asked throughout history by philosophers, theologians, and scientists alike. We may ask this question in different ways at different times in our lives. Sometimes we ask it when we feel lost and unsure of our purpose. Other times we ask it when we encounter challenges or difficulties that make us question our identity. Regardless of the circumstances that prompt the question, the answer lies in understanding our identity as children of God.

Your instinct is to seek your identity in the things around you, even while our society stresses the need to look inward. How we perceive ourselves greatly influences our actions and reactions. The way we see ourselves, how much we value ourselves, and how we feel about ourselves ultimately determine how we live. If we have a poor opinion of ourselves, we are more likely to behave badly. When we put ourselves in the victim role, we make it easier for others to take advantage of us. If we believe we are not creative, we will never generate original content. Like with anything we focus on, we come to believe we are what we focus on. If we have a positive mindset, we are more likely to achieve similar results to those we have in the past.

The first place your mind may wander to is your career. Investing your time and energy in pursuing your career can cause you to feel that it is a defining trait of who you are. After all, a profession that you are passionate about is going to take up most of your time and attention. Employment and careers are linked to various areas where we can look for our identity, including monetary success and social standing. But that's not all. We look to our romantic partners, physical attributes, academic achievements, and public profiles for validation of our identity as well.

All these may feel like sturdy foundations, but none of them are permanent. There is no guarantee that any of them will remain the same. You're setting yourself up for a world of hurt if you try to define yourself by things like money, fame, looks, and power. If you lose your job unexpectedly, you may start to doubt your decisions. Even if it's not true, just one bit of rumor about you can ruin your reputation. As you age, you'll naturally start to look different.

But God does not change. You can count on him. He has never changed; he always remains the same. Putting your faith in Him guarantees you'll never be let down since He's always been reliable.

For example, saying "I am a Christian," "I am religious," or "I am spiritual" only describes a small part of who you are; God must be at the center of your self-definition. Learning who God is and what He says about Himself and you is the first step in discovering your identity in Him. Who God is shaping you into in His likeness is at the heart of who you are.

Knowing who we are in Christ is not only important for our spiritual growth and well-being, but it also affects how we interact with the world around us. When we know who we are in Christ, we can live with confidence and purpose, knowing that we are part of something greater than ourselves.

So, who are we as Christians? We are children of God, new creations in Christ, ambassadors of Christ, part of the body of Christ, and called to holiness. These are just a few of the many aspects of our identity in Christ. Let us look at them in detail.

WE ARE CHILDREN OF GOD.

So, who are we as Christians? Firstly, we are children of God John 1:12 confirms this:

John 1:12, "Yet to all who did receive him, to those who believed in his name, he gave the right to become children of God."

This means that when we put our faith in Jesus Christ, we become part of God's family. We are adopted into His kingdom and have a new identity as His sons and daughters.

As children of God, we have a unique and special relationship with our Heavenly Father. This relationship is not based on anything we have done or achieved but, on the love, and grace of God. When we put our faith in Jesus Christ, we become part of God's family and are adopted as His sons and daughters.

This adoption into God's family is not just a legal transaction but a deep and personal relationship. We can come to God as our loving Father, knowing that He cares for us and desires the best for our lives. In fact, Jesus often referred to God as "Abba," which means "Father" in Aramaic, a term of endearment and intimacy.

As children of God, we have the privilege of being able to call upon our Heavenly Father for help, guidance, and comfort. We can trust that He hears our prayers and will always be with us, no matter what we are facing.

Matthew 7:11, "If you, then, though you are evil, know how to give good gifts to your children, how much more will your Father in heaven give good gifts to those who ask him!"

Being a child of God also means that we have a new identity. Our identity is no longer based on our past mistakes or our external appearances but on who we are in Christ. We are now part of a new family with a new inheritance and a new destiny.

Romans 8:16-17 "The Spirit himself testifies with our spirit that we are God's children. Now if we are children, then we are heirs—heirs of God and co-heirs with Christ, if indeed we share in his sufferings in order that we may also share in his glory."

This new identity as children of God gives us a sense of purpose and meaning in life. We are not just living for ourselves but for God and His purposes. We are part of a larger family and a larger story that God is unfolding in the world.

Being a child of God is central to our identity as Christians. It is a relationship based on God's love and grace, giving us a new sense of identity and purpose in life. As we continue to grow in our relationship with God, may we live our lives as His beloved children, trusting in His love and grace and seeking to serve Him in all that we do?

DO YOU SEE WHAT I'M SAYING

WE ARE NEW CREATIONS IN CHRIST

Secondly, we are new creations in Christ.

> *2 Corinthians 5:17, "Therefore, if anyone is in Christ, the new creation has come: The old has gone, the new is here!"*

This means that when we accept Jesus as our Lord and Savior, we are made new. Our old selves, with all of our sins and brokenness, are replaced with a new self-made in Christ's image. When we accept Jesus Christ as our Lord and Savior, we are born again and become new creations in Him.

This new creation is not just a superficial change but a transformation of our entire being. Our old self, with its sinful desires and selfish ways, is put to death, and we are raised to new life in Christ.

> *Romans 6:4, "We were therefore buried with him through baptism into death in order that, just as Christ was raised from the dead through the glory of the Father, we too may live a new life."*

This new life in Christ is characterized by righteousness, holiness, and obedience to God's will. As we grow in our relationship with Christ, we are transformed from the inside out, with our thoughts, attitudes, and behaviors becoming more and more aligned with God's perfect will.

> *Ephesians 4:22-24, "You were taught, with regard to your former way of life, to put off your old self, which is being corrupted by its deceitful desires; to be made new in the attitude of your minds; and to put on the new self, created to be like God in true righteousness and holiness."*

Being a new creation in Christ also means that we have a new purpose in life. We are no longer living for ourselves but for God and His purposes.

> *2 Corinthians 5:15 says, "And he died for all, that those who live should no longer live for themselves but for him who died for them and was raised again."*

This new purpose in life is not just for our benefit but for the benefit of others as well. We are called to love and serve others, just as Christ loved and served us.

Galatians 5:13, "You, my brothers and sisters, were called to be free. But do not use your freedom to indulge the flesh; rather, serve one another humbly in love."

Being a new creation in Christ is central to our identity as Christians. It is a transformational process that begins when we accept Christ as our Lord and Savior and continues throughout our lives as we grow in our relationship with Him. May we embrace this new identity and purpose in life, living as new creations in Christ and seeking to love and serve others for His glory.

WE ARE AMBASSADORS OF CHRIST.

As Christians, we are called to be ambassadors of Christ, representing Him and His message of reconciliation to the world.

2 Corinthians 5:20, "We are therefore Christ's ambassadors, as though God were making his appeal through us. We implore you on Christ's behalf: Be reconciled to God."

Being an ambassador of Christ means that we are His representatives, reflecting His character and communicating His message to those around us. Just as an ambassador represents a country and its values, we represent Christ and His kingdom. This means that our lives should reflect the values of the kingdom of God, such as love, humility, grace, and justice.

Our role as ambassadors of Christ also includes sharing the message of the gospel with others. We are called to be witnesses to the truth of who Christ is and what He has done for us.

Acts 1:8, "But you will receive power when the Holy Spirit comes on you; and you will be my witnesses in Jerusalem, and in all Judea and Samaria, and to the ends of the earth."

This witness is not just through our words but also our actions. We are called to live lives demonstrating the gospel's reality and transforming power.

DO YOU SEE WHAT I'M SAYING

Matthew 5:16, "Let your light shine before others, that they may see your good deeds and glorify your Father in heaven."

Being an ambassador of Christ is not always easy, as it may involve facing opposition, persecution, or rejection. However, we can take comfort in knowing that we are not alone in this task. We have the Holy Spirit within us, empowering us to live and speak boldly for Christ.

John 14:26, "But the Advocate, the Holy Spirit, whom the Father will send in my name, will teach you all things and will remind you of everything I have said to you."

Being an ambassador of Christ is a central aspect of our identity as Christians. We are called to represent Him and His message of reconciliation to the world through our words and actions. May we embrace this calling, relying on the power of the Holy Spirit and seeking to live and speak boldly for Christ for the sake of His kingdom and glory.

WE ARE PART OF THE BODY OF CHRIST

Fourthly, we are part of the body of Christ.

1 Corinthians 12:27, "Now you are the body of Christ, and each one of you is a part of it."

1 Corinthians 12:12-14, "Just as a body, though one, has many parts, but all its many parts forms one body, so it is with Christ. For we were all baptized by one Spirit so as to form one body—whether Jews or Gentiles, slave or free—and we were all given the one Spirit to drink. Even so, the body is not made up of one part but of many."

As Christians, we are not just individual believers, but we are also part of the larger body of Christ. Being part of the body of Christ means that we are united with other believers in Christ, sharing a common purpose and mission. We are called to love and serve one another, just as Christ loved and served us, as Paul writes in 1 Corinthians 12:25-27.

DR. SHAWN M. NICHOLSON

1 Corinthians 12:25-27, "so that there should be no division in the body, but that its parts should have equal concern for each other. If one part suffers, every part suffers with it; if one part is honored, every part rejoices with it. Now you are the body of Christ, and each one of you is a part of it."

This unity is not just a human effort but also a spiritual reality. As believers, we have all been baptized by the Holy Spirit into one body and share in the same Spirit. This means that we are all connected to Christ and to one another, and we are all called to use our unique gifts and talents for the benefit of the body.

Being part of the body of Christ also means that we are not just isolated individuals but part of a larger mission to bring the gospel to the world. We are called to work together, using our different gifts and abilities, to build up the body and to reach out to those who do not yet know Christ.

Being part of the body of Christ is a central aspect of our identity as Christians. We are called to be united with other believers, using our unique gifts and talents for the benefit of the body and for the sake of the gospel. May we embrace this identity, seeking to love and serve one another and work together to advance the kingdom of God for His glory and the good of all.

WE ARE CALLED TO HOLINESS

As Christians, we are called to live lives of holiness, set apart for God's purposes. We are to strive for holiness in all we do, seeking to be more like Christ daily.

In 1 Peter 1:15-16, the Apostle Peter writes, "But just as he who called you is holy, so be holy in all you do; for it is written: 'Be holy because I am holy.'"

To be holy means to be set apart for God, dedicated to His purposes, and committed to following His ways. It means that our lives should reflect His character, values and that we should strive to live in a pleasing way.

Holiness is not just a matter of outward behavior; it also involves our inner attitudes and motivations.

Matthew 5:8 says, "Blessed are the pure in heart, for they will see God."

This purity of heart involves a sincere desire to please God and to live in obedience to His commands, even when it may be difficult or unpopular. Living a holy life also means that we must avoid sin and temptation.

Romans 6:12-13, "Therefore do not let sin reign in your mortal body so that you obey its evil desires. Do not offer any part of yourself to sin as an instrument of wickedness, but rather offer yourselves to God as those who have been brought from death to life; and offer every part of yourself to him as an instrument of righteousness."

However, holiness is not something that we can achieve on our own. We need the power of the Holy Spirit to help us live a holy life.

Galatians 5:16, "So I say, walk by the Spirit, and you will not gratify the desires of the flesh."

When we submit to the Holy Spirit and allow Him to work in us, He empowers us to overcome sin and to live a life that honors God.

Being called to holiness is a central aspect of our identity as Christians. We are called to live lives that are set apart for God's purposes, reflecting His character and values and striving to avoid sin and temptation. May we embrace this calling, relying on the power of the Holy Spirit to help us live holy lives that honor God and bring glory to His name.

OUR IMAGE IN CHRIST

Our image in Christ reflects who He is and what He has done for us. The Bible teaches us that we were created in the image of God and that we were created for a purpose.

When we say that our image is created by God, we are affirming the biblical truth that humans are not simply the result of random chance or evolution but that we are intentionally and purposefully created by a loving God.

Genesis 1:27 says, "So God created man in his own image, in the image of God he created him; male and female he created them."

This verse emphasizes that humans are created in the image of God, which means that we have inherent worth and value because we reflect something of God's nature and character.

This truth has significant implications for how we view ourselves and others. If we are created in the image of God, it means that we are not accidents or mistakes but that we are intentional creations of a loving God. It means that we have inherent worth and value, regardless of our circumstances, our achievements, or our appearance. It means that our identity is not based on what we do or what we have but on who we are as creations of God. Let's look at what it means to have God's image.

WE ARE LOVED

Firstly, our image in Christ means that we are loved. The Bible tells us that God loved us so much that He sent His only Son to die for us (John 3:16). This is the ultimate expression of love, and it is a love that we do not deserve. We were once sinners, separated from God, but through Christ, we have been reconciled to Him (2 Corinthians 5:18-19). Knowing that we are loved by God, despite our shortcomings gives us a sense of security and peace that nothing in this world can offer.

WE ARE FORGIVEN

Secondly, our image in Christ means that we are forgiven. When we accept Jesus as our Lord and Savior, our sins are forgiven and made clean (1 John 1:9). This means that we no longer must carry the burden of guilt and shame. We can approach God with confidence, knowing that we have been made righteous through Christ (2 Corinthians 5:21). This is a powerful truth that can transform our lives and our relationships with others.

WE ARE CHOSEN

Thirdly, our image in Christ means that we are chosen. The Bible tells us that before the foundation of the world, God chose us to be His children (Ephesians 1:4-5). This means that we have a purpose and a destiny that has been ordained by God. We are not accidents or mistakes; we are intentional creations of a loving Father. Knowing that we are chosen by God gives us a sense of significance and purpose that cannot be found in anything else.

WE ARE EMPOWERED

Fourthly, our image in Christ means that we are empowered. Through the Holy Spirit, we have been given the power to live a life that is pleasing to God (Acts 1:8). We no longer have to rely on our strength and abilities; we have access to the power of God. This means we can overcome sin, temptation, and life's challenges. We can live a life that honors God and brings Him glory.

WE ARE CALLED TO BE LIKE HIM

Finally, our image in Christ means that we are called to be like Him. As Christians, we are called to follow in the footsteps of Jesus (1 Peter 2:21). This means that we are to love others, serve others, and live a life that is pleasing to God. We are called to be salt and light in the world, to bring hope and healing to those who are hurting. Our image in Christ is not just about who we are but about who we are becoming.

OUR IDENTITY IN CHRIST

It's important to remember that our identity in Christ is not based on anything we have done or achieved. It is purely based on the grace of God and the work of Jesus Christ on the cross. We don't have to strive to earn our identity or prove ourselves to God. We are already loved and accepted by Him, just as we are.

Some people identify with their line of work. They will make claims such as, "I'm a businessman," or "I'm a doctor," among other similar statements. However, their occupation does not define who they are; rather, it describes what they do. Some people associate themselves with the illness that is destroying their bodies. They will say things such as, "I have ADD," "I am bipolar," or "I have diabetes."

A lot has been said above about our identity, but I just need to add some things. When we have a true understanding of our identity in Christ — that is, who we are because of Him — it causes a change in the way that we think about and approach life.

Death and destruction were our inevitable ends before we were saved by Jesus Christ. But ever since we accepted Him, we have been assured of eternal life in Christ.

> *1 John 2:25, And this is what he promised us—eternal life.*

Before the coming of Christ, our fate was to be one of hopelessness, degradation, and poverty. But, because of Christ, we are meant to not only have life but to have an abundant amount of it.

> *John 10:10, The thief comes only to steal and kill and destroy; I have come that they may have life and have it to the full.*

Our identity, then, ought to be found in Christ alone. Because of Jesus, we have a purpose in this world.

Have you ever considered the possibility that God changes people's identities in response to their service to Him? They had a distorted view of themselves, but God showed them the truth about who they were. Gideon was subjected to these occurrences. In order to protect himself from the Midianites, he threshed his wheat while hiding inside a winepress. He was afraid that if the Midianites saw him threshing grain, they would seize what little possessions he did have.

One day the angel of the Lord appeared to Gideon in Judges 6:12.

DO YOU SEE WHAT I'M SAYING

Judges 6:12, When the angel of the Lord appeared to Gideon, he said, "The Lord is with you, mighty warrior."

Gideon's behavior was completely unfit for a courageous fighter! Despite this, he proceeded to save the Israelites after he gained a true understanding of how God viewed him.

A man's identity is so important to God that he had to change Abram's name. Abram and Sarai couldn't have children. The same way he changed Sarai's name. If this identity change does not happen, the promise of Isaac will not be fulfilled.

Gen. 17:5, No longer will you be called Abram; your name will be Abraham, for I have made you a father of many nations.

Gen. 17:15, God also said to Abraham, "As for Sarai your wife, you are no longer to call her Sarai; her name will be Sarah.

This is to tell us the impotence of identity to God and the fulfillment of destiny to humans.

However, our identity can be distorted by sin. When Adam and Eve sinned in the Garden of Eden, their sin had consequences not only for themselves but for all of humanity. Sin has marred our identity as image-bearers of God, and we are now separated from Him.

Romans 3:23, for all have sinned and fall short of the glory of God.

But the good news is that God has provided a way for us to be reconciled to Him through faith in Jesus Christ.

Romans 6:23, For the wages of sin is death, but the gift of God is eternal life in[a] Christ Jesus our Lord.

But as Christians, our identity is no longer defined by our sins or the world around us. Instead, our identity is now found in Christ. When we put our faith in Jesus, we become new creations. We are no longer defined by our past mistakes or our current circumstances. Instead, we are defined by our relationship with Christ.

DR. SHAWN M. NICHOLSON

Our identity in Christ means that we are now children of God. We are adopted into His family and have access to all the privileges that come with being a part of His family. We are now heirs of God and co-heirs with Christ. Our identity in Christ also means that we have been given the Holy Spirit to guide us and empower us to live a life that is pleasing to God.

> *Galatians 5:22-23, But the fruit of the Spirit is love, joy, peace, forbearance, kindness, goodness, faithfulness, gentleness, and self-control. Against such things, there is no law.*

As Christians, we are called to live considering our identity in Christ. This means that we are to reflect His nature in our thoughts, words, and actions. We are to love God with all our heart, soul, mind, and strength and love our neighbors as ourselves. We are to seek first the kingdom of God and His righteousness.

OUR INTEGRITY

Integrity is one of the core values of our identity in Christ. It is a word that means being honest, upright, and adhering to moral principles that protect our image and who we are. Integrity is doing the right thing, even when nobody is watching, when you are the only one that has access to the church account, when everything is in your care, and you choose to do the right thing even if nobody is there, knowing God is ever-present.

Last week I went to a store to buy some things, while the storeowner was still attending to me, a lady was leaving out the store while I was entering, came back with the store owner's phone saying she had taking it with her, and was almost home when she realized she had it. Everybody was surprised by her action, considering how expensive the phone was. She could have chosen not to return the phone since the store owner didn't know the phone was with gone, but she portrayed the true image of God.

I believe that we are created in the image of God and we have inherent values and dignity that should be respected and protected. Our identity is not determined by our accomplishments, material possessions, or social status. Instead, our identity is rooted in the fact that we are children of God, who loves us unconditionally.

Although, living a life of integrity is not easy. We live in a world that often promotes dishonesty, greed, and selfishness. We are bombarded with messages telling us to put our needs and desires first, even if it means compromising our values and hurting others in the process.

But, as Christians, we are called to live differently. We are called to be a light in the darkness, to stand for truth and justice, and to love our neighbors as ourselves. This requires us to have integrity in all areas of our lives.

Integrity starts with our relationship with God. We cannot have integrity in our interactions with others if we do not have integrity in our relationship with God. This means that we must be honest with God about our thoughts, feelings, and actions. We must confess our sins, ask for forgiveness, and seek to live in a way that honors God.

Integrity also requires us to be honest with ourselves. We must be willing to examine our motives and desires and be willing to admit when we are wrong. This can be challenging, as it requires humility and vulnerability. However, it is essential if we want to live a life that is pleasing to God.

Integrity is also demonstrated in our relationships with others. We must be truthful, reliable, and trustworthy in our interactions with others. This means keeping our promises, being transparent about our intentions, and treating others with respect and kindness.

Furthermore, integrity requires us to be good stewards of the resources that God has given us. This includes our time, talents, and finances. We must be honest in our business dealings and use our resources in a way that honors God and benefits others.

Integrity is an essential aspect of our identity in Christ. It reflects our relationship with God, our relationship with ourselves, and our relationship with others. Living a life of integrity requires us to be honest, transparent, and accountable. It requires us to put the needs of others before our own and to seek to honor God in all that we do. As Christians, let us strive to live a life of integrity so that we may be a light in the darkness and a testimony to God's love and grace.

CHAPTER TWO

WHOSE WE ARE

As Christians, we believe that our existence is not a mere coincidence or a product of chance. We believe that we were intentionally created by God and that we are made in His image. The question of "whose are we" is a fundamental one that helps us understand our identity, purpose, and value as human beings.

In the book of Genesis, we read about how God created the first man, Adam, and how He formed him from the dust of the ground and breathed into his nostrils the breath of life.

> *Genesis 2:7, Then the Lord God formed a man from the dust of the ground and breathed into his nostrils the breath of life, and the man became a living being.*

This act of creation shows us that we are not just physical beings but also spiritual beings with a purpose and destiny.

So, whose are we? As Christians, we belong to God. We are His children, and He has given us a purpose and a mission. Our identity is rooted in Him, and we are called to live our lives in a way that reflects His love and grace.

We are created to have a relationship with God and to fulfill His purpose for our lives. Jesus Christ, the Son of God, came to earth to show us what it means to live a life that pleases God, and He also gave His life as a sacrifice for our sins so that we could be reconciled to God and have eternal life.

The Bible teaches us that we are not our own but that we belong to God.

DR. SHAWN M. NICHOLSON

1 Corinthians 6:19-20, "Do you not know that your body is a temple of the Holy Spirit within you, whom you have from God? You are not your own, for you were bought with a price. So, glorify God in your body."

This is a reminder to us that we were purchased by God through the sacrifice of Jesus Christ and that we are now called to honor God with our bodies and our lives.

Our identity as Christians is rooted in our relationship with God. We are not defined by our accomplishments, possessions, or relationships but by our relationship with our Creator.

John 1:12-13, "But to all who did receive him, who believed in his name, he gave the right to become children of God, who were born, not of blood nor of the will of the flesh nor of the will of man, but of God."

When we understand that we belong to God, it changes the way we view ourselves and the world around us. We begin to see ourselves as valuable and loved by God, and we also begin to see others in the same way. We are called to love our neighbors as ourselves and to treat others with the same love and respect that God has shown us.

Mark 12:31, The second is this: 'Love your neighbor as yourself.' There is no commandment greater than these."

In today's world, it can be easy to lose sight of where we belong and to be pulled in different directions by the pressures of society. But as Christians, we have a firm foundation in Christ, and we can hold fast to the truth of who we are and whose we are.

At first glance, it may seem like an obvious answer. We belong to God, right? But have we truly internalized this truth and let it shape our lives? It's easy to get caught up in the day-to-day busyness and forget the big picture. So, let's take a moment to reflect on this question and delve deeper into what it means to belong to God.

DO YOU SEE WHAT I'M SAYING

WHAT IT MEANS TO BELONG TO GOD

As Christians, we know that our identity is found in Christ. We have been bought with a price and belong to God. This truth should shape how we live our lives, our decisions, and how we treat others. As we go through

life, we need to understand that we are children of God, created in His image, and called to live our lives in a way that brings glory to Him. let's look at what it means to belong to God below:

WE BELONG TO GOD BECAUSE HE CREATED US

The fact that God created us is a foundational truth that forms the basis of our identity as human beings. The Bible teaches us that God created us in His image and likeness, which means that we are unique and special creations. This truth should give us a sense of worth and dignity and a responsibility to live in a way that reflects our Creator.

One of the ways that we can honor God as our Creator is by taking care of His creation. God has entrusted us with the stewardship of the earth, and we are called to be good caretakers of it. This means that we should be mindful of our impact on the environment and how we treat other people and living beings.

Recognizing that God created us also means that we are accountable to Him for our actions. As the Creator, God has the right to set the standards for how we should live our lives, and we are responsible for living in obedience to His will. This truth should humble us and inspire us to seek His guidance and wisdom in all aspects of our lives.

Acknowledging that God created us also means that we have a purpose. God created us for a reason, and we should seek to understand and fulfill that purpose. This purpose may involve our careers, relationships, or other areas of our lives. By seeking God's will and purpose for our lives, we can find true fulfillment and joy.

Ultimately, recognizing that we belong to God because He created us should shape how we view ourselves, our environment, and our relationship with God. It should inspire us to live in obedience to His will, be good stewards of His creation, and seek to fulfill His purpose for our lives.

WE BELONG TO GOD BECAUSE WE ARE HIS CHILDREN

One of the most profound truths in Christianity is that we belong to God because we are His children. This means that we have a close, personal relationship with God as our Father and are part of His family. This relationship was made possible through the sacrifice of Jesus Christ on the cross, which reconciled us to God and made us the heirs of His kingdom.

As God's children, we have the privilege of approaching Him with confidence and receiving His love and guidance. We can come to Him with our fears, doubts, and struggles, knowing that He cares for us and will provide for our needs.

Matthew 7:11, "If you, then, though you are evil, know how to give good gifts to your children, how much more will your Father in heaven give good gifts to those who ask him!"

Being God's children also means that we are responsible for living in a way that reflects our Father's character. We are called to love others, just as He loves us, and to live in obedience to His will.

1 John 3:1-2, "See what great love the Father has lavished on us, that we should be called children of God! And that is what we are! The reason the world does not know us is that it did not know him. Dear friends, now we are children of God, and what we will has not yet been made known. But we know that when Christ appears, we shall be like him, for we shall see him as he is."

Furthermore, being God's children gives us a sense of belonging and purpose. We are not alone in this world but part of a larger family that spans time and space. We are called to love and support one another and to share the good news of God's love with those who do not yet know Him. As we fulfill this purpose, we bring glory to our Father and participate in His work of redeeming the world.

Being God's children is a profound truth that should shape how we view ourselves, our relationship with God, and our purpose in this world. As His children, we have the privilege of approaching Him with confidence, the responsibility to live in obedience to His will, and the sense of belonging and purpose that comes from being part of His family.

WE BELONG TO GOD BECAUSE HE REDEEMED US

Another powerful truth in Christianity is that we belong to God because He redeemed us. The word "redeem" means to buy back or restore something that was lost or broken. In the Bible, we see that God redeemed us by sending His Son, Jesus Christ, to die on the cross for our sins and to rise again, conquering death and offering us eternal life. Through Jesus' sacrifice, we are made new and reconciled to God.

Colossians 1:13-14, "For he has rescued us from the dominion of darkness and brought us into the kingdom of the Son he loves, in whom we have redemption, the forgiveness of sins."

This redemption is not something we earn or deserve but rather a gift from God's grace and love for us.

Belonging to God through redemption means that we have a new identity in Christ. We are no longer defined by our past mistakes or failures but by our relationship with God. We are now children of God with a new purpose and a new hope.

2 Corinthians 5:17, "Therefore, if anyone is in Christ, the new creation has come: The old has gone, the new is here!"

Redemption also means that we have a new power to live the life God intended for us. Through the Holy Spirit, we have the power to resist sin and to live in a way that pleases God.

> *Romans 6:4, "We were therefore buried with him through baptism into death in order that, just as Christ was raised from the dead through the glory of the Father, we too may live a new life."*

Finally, belonging to God through redemption means that we have a new destiny. We are no longer bound for destruction but for eternal life in

heaven with God. Our salvation and eternal life are gifts from God, and nothing can take them away from us.

> *Ephesians 2:8-9, "For it is by grace you have been saved, through faith—and this is not from yourselves, it is the gift of God—not by works, so that no one can boast."*

Belonging to God through redemption is a powerful truth that should shape how we view ourselves, our relationship with God, and our purpose and destiny in this world. Through Jesus' sacrifice, we are made new, reconciled to God, and given a new identity, power, and destiny. We are now children of God with a new purpose and hope in life.

WE BELONG TO GOD BECAUSE HE HAS A PURPOSE FOR OUR LIVES.

Another significant truth in Christianity is that we belong to God because He has a purpose for our lives. God has a unique plan for each of us, and He has created us with specific gifts, talents, and abilities to fulfill that plan.

> *Jeremiah 29:11, it says, "For I know the plans I have for you," declares the Lord, "plans to prosper you and not to harm you, plans to give you hope and a future."*

Belonging to God through His purpose for our lives means that we have a sense of direction and meaning. We are not wandering in this world, but we have a clear goal and mission. Our purpose is not just to survive in this world but to make a positive impact and bring glory to God.

Ephesians 2:10, "For we are God's handiwork, created in Christ Jesus to do good works, which God prepared in advance for us to do."

Moreover, belonging to God through His purpose means that we are responsible for using our gifts and talents to serve others. Our purpose is not just about us but about how we can use our gifts to benefit others and bring them closer to God.

1 Peter 4:10, "Each of you should use whatever gift you have received to serve others, as faithful stewards of God's grace in its various forms."

Belonging to God through His purpose also means that we have a sense of accountability. We are not free to live our lives as we please, but we are accountable to God for how we use our time, talents, and resources. Our purpose is not just a privilege but also a responsibility that requires us to be faithful and obedient to God's will.

Romans 14:12, "So then, each of us will give an account of ourselves to God."

Belonging to God through His purpose is a significant truth that should shape how we view ourselves, our relationship with God, and our mission in this world. We have a sense of direction, meaning, and accountability through His purpose. We are called to use our gifts and talents to serve others and to bring them closer to God. Our purpose is not just a personal privilege but also a responsibility that requires us to be faithful and obedient to God's will.

CHAPTER THREE

WHY ARE WE HERE?

As Christians, we often ask ourselves, "Why are we here?" This fundamental question has puzzled humanity since the beginning of time. A question that has been asked by philosophers, theologians, and scientists alike. Some believe humans just "evolved" from nothing, which is not a good enough response. An atheist will say life has no purpose at all.

However, there IS a God who created us for a reason, and your life does have a meaning and purpose with him. Then discovering what that purpose is for you is of the utmost importance. And in I Peter 2:4-5, God reveals what that purpose is.

I Peter 2:4-5, As you come to him, the living Stone—rejected by humans but chosen by God and precious to him— you also, like living stones, are being built into a spiritual house to be a holy priesthood, offering spiritual sacrifices acceptable to God through Jesus Christ.

Some people even wonder, "Why are we even born if we are only going to die some 70 or 80 years later?" Is there nothing more to life than "Eat, drink, and be merry, for tomorrow we die?" If you think the universe came into being in a "Big Bang," that humans were developed from simple organisms like amoebas over millions of years, or that there is no Creator, then you are wrong. Even science is starting to acknowledge that the Earth is becoming older. Much like man, it is perishing and will not be around forever. Hence, questions like, "Why are we here?" arise in our minds.

From the beginning, God created everything, from stars to Earth to people to amoebas. According to the Bible, God made man and woman to reflect his own image, and he intended to have "fellowship" (companionship or friendship) with his creations when they were created. According to Genesis 1:1-28, God "blessed" Adam and Eve and let them "rule over the fish of the sea and the birds of the air and over every living creature that moves on the ground." Our purpose of being here is to care for the world. If we have a personal relationship with God, then being here will also provide us joy. However, we are also here to bring pleasure to God.

Living and dying are not the only two aspects of existence. Everyone is created in God's image, which means we have a personality and are able to love, laugh, feel, and think. This is because God is love. He does not want anyone to be destroyed, but he does wish for everyone to repent.

2 Peter 3:9, The Lord is not slow in keeping his promise, as some understand slowness. Instead, he is patient with you, not wanting anyone to perish, but everyone to come to repentance.

What is repentance, and why is it so crucial for our lives? Sin was brought into the world when the first man, Adam, disobeyed God and sinned. Because Adam's sin introduced death into the world, everyone eventually succumbed.

Romans 5:12, Therefore, just as sin entered the world through one man, and death through sin, and in this way, death came to all people, because all sinned.

Because God is holy and we are sinful, it is impossible for us to connect with him until we acknowledge that we are sinful by nature and have faith that through Jesus Christ, God has provided a method for us to transform our sinful nature through repentance. Only then can we have a relationship with God. To glorify God, to learn more about God, and to extend the blessings of this experience to as many people as possible while we are still on earth is the purpose for which we have been created here on earth, while our ultimate goal is to spend all of eternity in Heaven. This is only possible for us if we have placed our faith in Jesus to save us. Let us look at some of the reasons why we are here.

WHY GOD CREATED US

BE FRUITFUL AND MULTIPLY.

God created humanity to reproduce and fill the earth with life. This command to be fruitful and multiply is found in the book of Genesis, where God created Adam and Eve and gave them the responsibility to populate the earth.

Genesis 1:28, "God blessed them and said to them, 'Be fruitful and increase in number; fill the earth and subdue it.'"

This command is not just about physical reproduction but also about fulfilling God's plan for humanity. By multiplying and filling the earth with life, we are fulfilling God's purpose for us and contributing to His plan for the world.

DO YOU SEE WHAT I'M SAYING

As Christians, we believe that our purpose in life is to love and serve God and to love and serve others. By being fruitful and multiplying, we are creating new life and contributing to the well-being of the world around us.

"Be fruitful and multiply, fill the earth, and subdue it" This is both the proclamation of God's blessing and the duty that He is handing up to humanity. Other than man, other living creatures have been blessed with the ability to participate in the creation process of God of creating offspring, as seen in Genesis 1:22, 24-25.

But only to man was it given as a mandate not merely to populate the earth but also to dominate it. This doesn't mean only to have children but also to bring up godly children who can dominate the earth in the right way under God's authority. The planet is populated by humans, yet they are unable to dominate it because of their sinful procreation.

For us to be able to create godly children, every one of us will need to participate in evangelism. To fill the world and dominate it indicates that we must conquer Satan, the ruler of the earth, by rescuing people from his dominion of darkness and seeing them transferred to the kingdom of God's loving Son.

> *Col. 1:13, For he has rescued us from the dominion of darkness and brought us into the kingdom of the Son he loves,*

This is necessary for us to be able to fill the planet and subdue it. Unless they submit their lives to the authority of Jesus Christ, human beings will never be able to mirror the image of God, govern over His creation, or create godly children. This spiritual application is made by the author of Hebrews when he credits the words, "Here am I, and the children God has given me."

> *Heb. 2:13, And again, "I will put my trust in him." And again, he says, "Here am I, and the children God has given me."*

The gift of spiritual offspring, a fruit that endures for all of eternity, is one of God's most wonderful things to bestow on a person.

Being fruitful and multiplying is about fulfilling God's plan for our lives and contributing to the growth and flourishing of the world around us. It is a responsibility that should be carried out with love, care, and reverence for the gift of life that God has given us.

TO HAVE DOMINION

According to Christian belief, we are here and have been given dominion over the earth to fulfill God's plan for creation. God created the earth and everything in it, and He gave humans the responsibility to take care of it and use its resources in a responsible and sustainable way.

Having dominion over the earth is not just a matter of power or control but a call to serve God and care for His creation. This means being good stewards of the environment, using its resources wisely and sustainably, and caring for the animals and plants that share this planet with us.

As Christians, we believe that God has entrusted us with this responsibility, and we have a duty to fulfil it with integrity, wisdom, and respect. We are called to be caretakers of the earth, using its resources in a way that honors' God and benefits future generations.

Before the fall, man was the master of all creation. But after Satan succeeded in getting man to follow him, he established himself as the master of this world. For man to reclaim the position of dominion over this world that is rightfully his, he must first exercise dominion not only over the physical world but also over the spiritual powers of evil (Ephesians 6:10-20). To get this, we must first become a part of the body of Christ, who, because of His resurrection, now holds the position of dominion over all things (Eph. 1:19-23). This is the only way to obtain this status. As a result, a significant part of why we are here is to engage in spiritual combat with the aim of asserting Christ's supremacy over Satan and the armies he commands.

The practical meaning of the fact that we rule over creation is that we need to put on the entire armor of God and, most importantly, become a praying people (Ephesians 6:13-17, 18-19). When Peter discusses the duties of the husband and the woman in a marriage, he instructs the husband to respect his wife as a joint heir of the grace of life "so that your prayers may not be hindered."

1 Peter 3:7, Husbands, in the same way be considerate as you live with your wives and treat them with respect as the weaker partner and as heirs with you of the gracious gift of life, so that nothing will hinder your prayers.

This instruction is given to the husband when Peter discusses the responsibilities of the husband and the wife in a marriage. Therefore, via the power of prayer, we are to exercise authority not just in the church but also in our own homes, not only over all of creation but particularly the spiritual forces associated with darkness.

However, it's important to note that having dominion over the earth does not give us the right to exploit or abuse it. Instead, it calls us to exercise responsible stewardship over the earth, taking care of it and using its resources to benefit humanity and the environment.

We are here to fulfill God's plan for creation by being good stewards of the earth, using its resources in a responsible and sustainable way, and caring for the plants and animals that share this planet with us. As Christians, we believe having dominion over the earth is a call to serve God and care for His creation. This responsibility should be taken seriously and fulfilled with humility and respect.

Therefore, God placed humans on earth so that we might mirror His image and have dominion over creation.

TO REPLENISH THE WORLD

Genesis 1:28, And God blessed them, and God said unto them, be fruitful, and multiply, and replenish the earth, and subdue it: and have dominion over the fish of the sea, and over the fowl of the air, and over every living thing that moveth upon the earth.

DR. SHAWN M. NICHOLSON

Adam was entrusted with the responsibility of overseeing the earth after God created it. He subjected everything to him and gave him authority over everything, both living and non-living creatures. He was put in control of everything. When God instructed humans to "replenish the earth," the term "replenish" immediately suggests to me a few extremely significant ideas.

When God saw that the lovely world he had created had degenerated into an unorganized mess, he blessed man and saddled him with the responsibility of restoring it. To refill something also implies refurbishing it, replacing it, fixing it, or returning it to its previous state.

That indicates that something went awry; a demon out there had messed things up, and man was given the chance and obligation to rectify the situation. That is the glorious life that we have been called to live because of our faith in Christ: a life in which we have power, authority, blessings, and control over the world in which we live. The earth is ours to conquer and bring under our control.

Nevertheless, God did not command us to dominate one another on the earth in any way. Regarding one another, His desire is for us to walk in love.

> *1 John 4:7-8, Beloved, let us love one another: for love is of God; and everyone that loveth is born of God, and knoweth God. He that loveth not knoweth not God; for God is love.*

In the same way that you walk in dominion and control over the universe and all its components, over the whims of nature, He tells you to "love one another." Because every one of us was created in the image and likeness of our heavenly Father, you shouldn't try to exercise an excessive amount of control over other people.

TO RECONCILE THE WORLD WITH GOD

DO YOU SEE WHAT I'M SAYING

2 Corinthians 5:18 – 21, All this is from God, who reconciled us to himself through Christ and gave us the ministry of reconciliation: that God was reconciling the world to himself in Christ, not counting people's sins against them. And he has committed to us the message of reconciliation. We are, therefore, Christ's ambassadors, as though God were making his appeal through us. We implore you on Christ's behalf: Be reconciled to God. God made him who had no sin to be sin for us, so that in him we might become the righteousness of God.

Paul explains to us in the book of 2 Corinthians what our function is as Christians worldwide. It is incumbent upon us to serve as Christ's representatives here on earth, demonstrating his compassion for our fellow man in accordance with the teachings of the gospel. Others may also be reconciled to God through faith in Christ, and God will use us to communicate the gospel of reconciliation with them. Just as we were reconciled to God by faith in Christ, so too can others be reconciled to God.

To live according to the blueprint God has laid out for our life requires that we imitate the apostles' behavior by preaching the gospel to others and leading by example in terms of our good deeds. When Jesus instructed his apostles to have faith in God when they assumed leadership roles among men and women, so too must we have faith in God so that he might guide us in making moral decisions.

Being a Christian entail more than just coming to church on Sundays; according to God's design, Christians are to serve as ambassadors for Christ twenty-four hours a day, seven days a week, 365 days a year. Our love for Christ ought to be obvious in our hearts, and it ought to find expression in both our words and our actions.

WE WERE BORN TO SERVE

Galatians 6:10, Therefore, as we have the opportunity, let us do good to all people, especially to those who belong to the family of believers.

DR. SHAWN M. NICHOLSON

Upon contemplating God's will for our lives, many ask questions like, "What about my plans for my life?" We make up stories in our heads about the people we are meant to marry, the jobs we are supposed to do, the places we are supposed to live, and any number of other aspects of life that we believe would please us.

We fail to remember that God has a far better plan for us than we have for ourselves. Throughout the Bible, God reveals to us that our primary purpose in life is to serve him. This life of service requires that we love other people and pay attention to the things they need. God instructs us to treat one another with kindness, compassion, and forgiveness.

> *Ephesians 4:32, Be kind and compassionate to one another, forgiving each other, just as in Christ God forgave you.*

Serving others in the way God established for us is a part of God's plan for us. In the story that Jesus told, the Good Samaritan helped a man who was in need. We, too, must follow Christ's example and be obedient in assisting those in the greatest need of our help.

TO VALUE PEOPLE

> *John 3:16, For God so loved the world that he gave his one and only Son, that whoever believes in him shall not perish but have eternal life.*

Even though we have been given the task of representing Christ as ambassadors in this world, the will of God for our lives goes far beyond what we accomplish in this earthly world. He has invited us all to return to his realm and spend eternity with him there. In the Gospel of John, we see that God's plan for us is motivated by love; this love is so powerful that God was willing to give up his one and only Son, Jesus Christ, to save us from our sins.

Even while we may be concerned about the future, such as whether we will find work or whether we will find that one special someone, God is far more concerned about us. Because God loves us so much, our deliverance from sin and death is central to his life plan. Even though we have all sinned and come up short of the glory that God deserves, the Holy Spirit compels us to accept God's love and spread it to others around us.

TO GLORIFY GOD AND TO ENJOY HIM FOREVER

Our ultimate purpose is to bring honor and praise to God through our lives and to find joy and fulfillment in Him. This purpose is not limited to our

actions within the church or during times of worship but extends to every area of our lives - our work, relationships, hobbies, and more.

> *Revelation 4:11, "You are worthy, our Lord and God, to receive glory and honor and power, for you created all things, and by your will, they were created and have their being."*

Glorifying God means acknowledging His greatness and worthiness and living in a way that reflects His character and values. This includes loving and serving others, obeying His commands, and sharing the good news of His salvation with others.

Enjoying God means finding joy and satisfaction in our relationship with Him. This comes from praying and worship, reading and studying His Word, and experiencing His presence in our lives.

> *Psalm 16:11, "You make known to me the path of life; you will fill me with joy in your presence, with eternal pleasures at your right hand."*

However, our ability to fulfill this purpose was marred by sin. Adam and Eve's disobedience in the Garden of Eden resulted in a broken relationship between God and humanity. But God did not leave us without hope. He sent His Son, Jesus Christ, to reconcile us to Himself and restore us to our intended purpose.

Through faith in Christ, we can live in a way that brings glory to God and find true joy in Him.

> *Colossians 3:17, "And whatever you do, in word or deed, do everything in the name of the Lord Jesus, giving thanks to God the Father through him."*

DR. SHAWN M. NICHOLSON

Understanding our purpose as Christians can bring clarity and direction to our lives. We are not aimlessly wandering through this world but rather have a specific calling to fulfill. As we seek to glorify God and enjoy Him forever, we can trust that He will guide us and provide for us.

Glorifying God and enjoying Him forever form the foundation of a fulfilling and purposeful life. Only through a deep and meaningful relationship with Him can we truly find joy, peace, and fulfillment in life.

CHAPTER FOUR

POWER VS AUTHORITY

God has given you the power and the authority to stand against Satan and his destructive works. He has provided the armor, but it is your responsibility as a believer to put on that armor and stand against the devil. James 4:7 says, YOU resist the devil, and he will flee from YOU.

The armor and the weapons are at your disposal. God is there with you to back His Word; but all is worthless unless you take your position of authority and assume the responsibility to use what He has provided. You have the power and the authority to take the Word of God, the name of Jesus, and the power of the Holy Spirit and run Satan out of your affairs. Don't pray and ask God to fight Satan for you. You are the one in authority. Take your responsibility and speak directly to Satan yourself and stand your ground firmly. He will flee!

Power and authority are two terms often used interchangeably, but they are not the same. Power refers to the ability to control or influence others, while authority refers to the right to do so. In the context of the Christian faith, power and authority have different meanings and implications.

In the Bible, power is often associated with physical strength or force. The word "power" is used to describe an army's might or an individual's strength. In the New Testament, the Greek word for power is "dunamis," which is where we get the word "dynamite." This word emphasizes the explosive force of power.

On the other hand, authority refers to the right to exercise power or control over others. In the Bible, authority is often associated with God. God has the ultimate authority over all things, and He has delegated authority to individuals and institutions.

> *Romans 13:1-2, "Let every person be subject to the governing authorities. For there is no authority except from God, and those that exist have been instituted by God. Therefore, whoever resists the authorities resists what God has appointed, and those who resist will incur judgment."*

This difference is important because power can be misused, while authority cannot. Power can be gained through force or coercion, but authority can only be given by those with the power to delegate it. For example, a king may have the power to rule a nation, but his authority comes from God.

In the Christian faith, power can be a dangerous thing. The desire for power can lead to pride, arrogance, and a lack of concern for others. This is why Jesus taught His disciples to use their authority in service to others, not to gain power or control over them.

> *Matthew 20:25-28, "You know that the rulers of the Gentiles lord it over them, and their high officials exercise authority over them. Not so with you. Instead, whoever wants to become great among you must be your servant, and whoever wants to be first must be your slave— just as the Son of Man did not come to be served, but to serve, and to give his life as a ransom for many."*

Let's look at some examples in the bible. In the book of Exodus, we see Pharaoh exerting his power over the Israelites by enslaving them and subjecting them to harsh labor. But when God called Moses to lead the Israelites out of Egypt, Moses was given the authority by God to confront Pharaoh and demand the Israelites' release. Moses didn't have the power to overthrow Pharaoh's rule, but he had the authority given to him by God to speak on His behalf and lead the Israelites out of Egypt.

King Saul was the first king of Israel and had the power and authority to rule over the people. However, when he disobeyed God, God took away his authority to rule, and He chose David to be the next king. David was anointed by God, and he had the authority given to him by God to lead and protect the people of Israel. Despite being pursued by Saul and his armies, David did not use his power to retaliate or harm Saul. He respected Saul's authority as the king until Saul's death.

The Pharisees were religious leaders in Jesus' time, and they had the power to interpret and enforce the religious laws of the time. However, when Jesus began His ministry, He showed that He had the authority given to Him by God to teach and heal the people. He did not use His power to overthrow the Pharisees or gain control over them. Instead, He spoke the truth in love and challenged their legalistic approach to religion.

In these examples, we see that power and authority are not the same thing. Pharaoh had the power to enslave the Israelites, but Moses had the authority God gave him to lead them out of Egypt. King Saul had the power to rule over Israel, but David had the authority given to him by God to become the next king. The Pharisees had the power to interpret and enforce religious laws, but Jesus had the authority given to Him by God to teach and heal the people.

As Christians, we are called to use our authority in service to others, just as Moses, David, and Jesus did. We are not called to use our power to control or manipulate others. Instead, we are called to follow Jesus' example of humility and selflessness, using our authority to serve and love those around us. Here are some of the ways we can use our power and authority in a way that pleases God.

HOW TO USE POWER AND AUTHORITY IN A GODLY WAY

As Christians, we are called to use our power and authority in a way that honors God. This means using our power to serve others and to bring glory to God. It means recognizing that our authority comes from God and using it in a way that is consistent with His character and will. Let's dive into how we can achieve this:

DEVELOP A SERVANT'S HEART

Developing a servant's heart is an essential part of using power and authority in a godly way. This means putting the needs of others before our desires for power or control. It means being willing to sacrifice our comfort and convenience for the sake of others, as Jesus says in John 13:14-15.

John 13:14-15, "If I then, your Lord and Teacher, have washed your feet, you also ought to wash one another's feet. For I have given you an example, that you also should do just as I have done to you."

It involves shifting our focus from ourselves and our desires to the needs of others. Here are some ways that we can cultivate a servant's heart:

Follow the example of Jesus

Jesus is the ultimate example of a servant leader. He willingly laid down His life for others, and throughout His ministry, He consistently put the needs of others before His own. He taught His disciples to do the same, saying, "Whoever wants to become great among you must be your servant" (Matthew 20:26). Studying the life of Jesus and following His example is a crucial step in developing a servant's heart.

Practice humility

Humility is a key characteristic of a servant's heart. It means recognizing that we are not the center of the universe and that others are just as important as we are. We can practice humility by acknowledging our weaknesses and limitations, listening to others with an open mind, and being willing to learn from those who have less power or authority than we do.

Look for opportunities to serve

We can develop a servant's heart by actively seeking out opportunities to serve others. This might mean volunteering at a local charity, helping a neighbor in need, or simply listening to someone going through a difficult time. Serving others should become a regular part of our lives rather than something we do only when it is convenient or when we feel like it.

Practice gratitude

A grateful heart is a servant's heart. When we are grateful for what we have, we are more likely to want to share our blessings with others. We can cultivate gratitude by taking time each day to reflect on the good things in our lives, expressing our gratitude to God and others, and using our resources to help those less fortunate.

Practice forgiveness

Forgiveness is an essential aspect of a servant's heart. When we forgive others, we let go of our desire for power and control and show compassion and mercy to those who have wronged us. Forgiveness can be difficult, but it is a powerful way to serve others and demonstrate the love of Chris

As we follow the example of Jesus, practice humility, look for opportunities to serve, cultivate gratitude, and practice forgiveness, we will become more effective servants of God and better stewards of the power and authority He has entrusted to us.

SEEK THE WISDOM AND GUIDANCE OF GOD

Another way to use our power and authority godly is to seek God's wisdom and guidance. This involves seeking His will and guidance in all we do and relying on His strength and wisdom rather than our own.

> *Proverbs 3:5-6, "Trust in the Lord with all your heart and lean not on your own understanding; in all your ways submit to him, and he will make your paths straight."*

Here are some ways that we can cultivate a habit of seeking God's wisdom and guidance:

Prayer

Prayer is the most basic way to seek God's wisdom and guidance. It involves talking to God, pouring out our hearts to Him, and asking Him for direction in our lives. We can pray about anything and everything, from big decisions to small details. Jesus Himself taught us to pray,

> *Matthew 6:10, "Your kingdom come, your will be done, on earth as it is in heaven."*

This means asking God to guide us and show us His will in every area of our lives.

Scripture

The Bible is God's written Word, full of wisdom and guidance. Reading and studying the Bible is essential to seeking God's wisdom and guidance.

> *2 Timothy 3:16-17, "all Scripture is God-breathed and is useful for teaching, rebuking, correcting and training in righteousness, so that the servant of God may be thoroughly equipped for every good work."*

By immersing ourselves in the Bible, we can better understand God's character, His will for our lives, and His plan for the world.

The Holy Spirit

The Holy Spirit is the third person of the Trinity, and He is the one who guides us into all truth (John 16:13). As Christians, we have the Holy Spirit living within us, and we can rely on Him to give us wisdom and guidance in every situation. We can ask the Holy Spirit to discern us, help us understand God's will, and lead us in the right direction.

Wise Counsel

God often speaks to us through other people. We can seek the wisdom and guidance of godly friends, mentors, pastors, and counselors. When we seek the advice of wise and godly people, we can gain a different perspective and insight into our situation.

> *Proverbs 15:22, "Plans fail for lack of counsel, but with many advisers they succeed."*

Seeking the wisdom and guidance of God is an essential part of using power and authority in a godly way. By praying, reading, and studying the Bible, relying on the Holy Spirit, and seeking wise counsel, we can discern God's will for our lives and make decisions that honor Him. As we seek God's wisdom and guidance, we will become more effective servants of God and better stewards of the power and authority He has entrusted to us.

BEING HUMBLE AND SUBMITTING TO OTHERS

We can also godlily use our power and authority by being humble and submitting to others. This means recognizing that we are not the ultimate authority and that there are others who have knowledge, wisdom, and experience that we can learn from.

> *Philippians 2:3-4, Paul writes, "Do nothing out of selfish ambition or vain conceit. Rather, in humility value others above yourselves, not looking to your own interests but each of you to the interests of the others."*

It involves putting the needs of others before our own, recognizing our limitations and weaknesses, and showing respect and deference to those around us. Here are some ways that we can cultivate a habit of being humble and submitting to others:

Putting the needs of others first

One of the hallmarks of humility is putting the needs of others before our own. We should be willing to sacrifice our desires and ambitions for the sake of others, whether that means serving them, listening to them, or simply putting their needs ahead of our own.

Recognizing our limitations and weaknesses

Another aspect of humility is recognizing our limitations and weaknesses. We are not perfect, and we are not capable of doing everything on our own.

> *James 4:6, "God opposes the proud but shows favor to the humble."*

When we humble ourselves before God and acknowledge our need for Him, we can experience His grace and strength.

Showing respect and deference to others

Humility also involves showing respect and deference to those around us, especially those in positions of authority.

> *Romans 13:1, "Let everyone be subject to the governing authorities, for there is no authority except that which God has established."*

We should show respect and deference to our leaders, obeying the laws of the land or submitting to the authority of our bosses at work.

Practicing forgiveness and reconciliation

Finally, humility involves practicing forgiveness and reconciliation in our relationships with others. When wronged or hurt by someone else, it can be tempting to hold a grudge or seek revenge. But Jesus taught us to forgive others as we have been forgiven (Matthew 6:14-15). When we choose to forgive and reconcile with those who have wronged us, we demonstrate the humility and grace of Christ in our lives.

Being humble and submitting to others is an essential part of using power and authority in a godly way. By putting the needs of others first, recognizing our limitations and weaknesses, showing respect and deference to those in authority, and practicing forgiveness and reconciliation, we can cultivate a habit of humility and become more effective servants of God. As we follow the example of Christ, who humbled Himself and became a servant for our sake (Philippians 2:5-8), we will become better stewards of the power and authority God has given us.

SEEKING JUSTICE AND RIGHTEOUSNESS

We can use our power and authority godly by seeking justice and righteousness. This means using our power and authority to stand up for what is right, to defend the vulnerable and oppressed, and to promote justice and fairness.

> *Micah 6:8, "He has shown you, O mortal, what is good. And what does the Lord require of you? To act justly and to love mercy and to walk humbly with your God."*

As followers of Christ, we are called to stand up for what is right and just, defend the weak and vulnerable, and advocate for those oppressed or marginalized. Here are some ways that we can seek justice and righteousness:

Understanding God's heart for justice

DR. SHAWN M. NICHOLSON

God is a God of justice and righteousness. Throughout the Bible, we see that God cares deeply about the plight of the oppressed and marginalized and expects His people to do the same.

> *Micah 6:8, "He has shown you, O mortal, what is good. And what does the Lord require of you? To act justly and to love mercy and to walk humbly with your God."*

When we understand God's heart for justice, we are inspired to work for change and make a difference.

Advocating for the vulnerable

One way we can seek justice and righteousness is by advocating for the vulnerable. This includes speaking up for those who are voiceless, standing up against oppression and injustice, and defending the rights of the marginalized. When we advocate for the vulnerable, we are living out God's call to seek justice and righteousness.

> *Proverbs 31:8-9, "Speak up for those who cannot speak for themselves, for the rights of all who are destitute. Speak up and judge fairly; defend the rights of the poor and needy."*

Addressing systemic issues

Another way we can seek justice and righteousness is by addressing systemic issues that perpetuate injustice and oppression. This might involve working to change laws and policies that discriminate against certain groups or advocating for greater access to resources and opportunities for marginalized people. We can help create a more just and equitable society by addressing these underlying systemic issues.

Practicing personal righteousness

Finally, seeking justice and righteousness also involves practicing personal righteousness in our own lives. This means living according to God's standards of right and wrong and striving to be people of integrity and moral uprightness. When we live with personal righteousness, we set an example for others to follow and demonstrate our commitment to seeking justice and righteousness in all areas of life.

Psalm 106:3, "Blessed are those who act justly, who always do what is right."

Seeking justice and righteousness is a vital part of using power and authority in a godly way. By understanding God's heart for justice, advocating for the vulnerable, addressing systemic issues, and practicing personal righteousness, we can make a difference in the world and bring about positive change. As we seek to live out God's call to seek justice and righteousness, we can honor Him and reflect His love and compassion to those around us.

DR. SHAWN M. NICHOLSON

MESSAGE FROM THE AUTHOR

Thank you again for supporting me and my work! I trust you are enjoying reading and learning from this powerful resource. I am humbled you have allowed me to continue to live out my purpose.

L3 Publishing House, "Unleashing the Power of Words, One Book at a Time," has allowed me to live out my purpose in life, which is to PASS-I-ON®, through my writing.

As we pause at the halfway point of our transformative journey through the first four chapters—delving into the fundamental questions of who we are, whose we are, why we are here, and the profound power and authority bestowed upon us—it is now a moment to reflect, refocus, and reset.

This book, "Do You See What I'm Saying? Walking by Faith; Trusting God's Guidance Every Step of the Way," is for every believer. The first four chapters have been a compass, guiding you through the intricacies of your identity, purpose, and the immense power within you. Now, as you stand at this pivotal juncture, it is time to deepen your understanding of faith. Scripture reminds us that faith comes by hearing, and hearing by the Word of God.

Romans 10: 17 "So then faith cometh by hearing, and hearing by the word of God."

As we move forward into the second half, open your hearts and minds to absorb the wisdom that awaits you, embracing the path of faith and trusting God's guidance with every step we take.

~Dr. Shawn M. Nicholson

CHAPTER FIVE

HAVING FAITH IN GOD

Having Faith in God: Faith is a foundational concept in Christianity. It involves trusting in God's promises and character, even when we cannot see or understand His plans. Faith in God is the belief and trust that He is who He says He is and will do what He promises to do. This includes believing that God created the world, sent His son Jesus to die for our sins and that He will one day return to judge the living and the dead. It also involves trusting that God is loving, just, and all-powerful.

In Mark 11:22

"And Jesus answering saith unto them, Have faith in God."

Jesus teaches His disciples what is necessary to experience the power of God. The call of Jesus is simple: **Have faith in God**. Believe that He can do the impossible and go to Him in faith.

For we walk by faith, not by sight.
(2 Cor. 5:7 NKJV)

When God tells us to walk by faith and not by sight, He does not mean that we shouldn't look where we are going, He does not mean He doesn't want us to know, and He does not mean we live our lives not knowing what we are doing from one day to the next. What God does mean, is that we should walk (live) as He does - by faith (in His knowledge, in His wisdom), and trusting in Him.

Rom. 10:17 tells us faith comes from hearing His Word. John 1:1 tells us He is His Word. Therefore, when we hear His Word, we get His wisdom, His thinking, His knowledge, and His direction. Faith in God comes as we take the time to know Him, just as you take time to know your best friend, spouse, or some other person. When you take time to know someone, your confidence will grow in trusting that person, just by the experience you have with them.

That same principal will work with God. As you take time to know Him, He will reveal to you, His ways. Knowing God and having experience with Him will give you great faith in Him. He will share His wisdom with you, He will tell you things to come, and He will show you and give you more than you can imagine. But you must take the time to know Him to get in that position.

Faith is a foundational concept in Christianity. It involves trusting in God's promises and character, even when we cannot see or understand His plans.

DO YOU SEE WHAT I'M SAYING

Faith in God is the belief and trust that He is who He says He is and will do what He promises to do. This includes believing that God created the world, sent His son Jesus to die for our sins and that He will one day return to judge the living and the dead. It also involves trusting that God is loving, just, and all-powerful. According to Hebrews 11:1,

Hebrews 11:1, faith is "the substance of things hoped for, the evidence of things not seen."

To further elaborate on what he stated in verse one, he writes in verse 6:

Hebrews 11:6 "But without faith it is impossible to please God, for whoever comes to God must believe that He is, and that He is a rewarder of those who diligently seek Him."

Having faith in God's existence is only the first step. Although many people accept the possibility of a higher power, they choose not to dedicate their life to that power. Like everyone else, demons are certain God exists, yet they don't worship him. Having confidence in God is the first step in establishing a personal connection with the Creator, who seeks more than just our recognition of His presence.

Reading all of Hebrews 11 reveals that for each of the people that the writer highlights, it was their trust in God that ultimately led to a life of victory despite the difficulties they experienced. The apostle John writes in 1 John 5:4:

1 John 5:4, for everyone born of God overcomes the world. This is the victory that has overcome the world, even our faith.

There are several accounts in the Gospels of people who came to Jesus with various needs and how He helped them because of their faith.

In most circumstances, the things we go through enrich, enhance, challenge, cultivate, and bring to life our connection with God. Indeed, life itself is the school where faith is nurtured and developed.

Paul presents a story from Abraham and Sarah's lives to illustrate the importance of faith in our everyday life. Their desire for a child was the means through which God tested and strengthened their faith. Abraham and Sarah longed for a child despite their old age and having never had any children.

Who doesn't have at least a passing familiarity with the desires that lie deep inside the human heart? You must be itching to get that promotion finally you've been working so hard for. Yearning for healing that is so sorely needed, whether for ourselves or for a loved one we care about. Wishing with all your heart for a son or daughter to come back home to.

Having a strong desire for reconciliation even though it seems unlikely to ever occur. We hope that someone in a position of power and compassion would listen to our case on the fact that they screwed up and jumbled up our retirement pension benefits, mortgage loan, or rapidly increasing medical expenditures due to hospitalizations. We are longing for this person to hear our case.

Regardless of our backgrounds, we can all relate to the universal yearnings of the human heart when expectations are unmet, help isn't on the way, and the answer to our prayers hopes, and needs is postponed. Yes, God uses trials and tribulations to strengthen and deepen our faith.

Moreover, note Paul's opening remarks in Romans 1:17, where he lays out the standards by which we must live.

> *Romans 1:17, For in the gospel the righteousness of God is revealed—a righteousness that is by faith from first to last, just as it is written: "The righteous will live by faith."*

Our good deeds will not rescue us. Our success will not save us. Money is necessary to maintain creaturely duties and conveniences, but it cannot save us. We can only be saved and guaranteed eternal life with Christ by putting our trust in God.

Abraham and Sarah wanted a son, but they were becoming too old. They tried to fix things on their own, but that was against God's will. There are certain instances where it seems like no matter what we do, and the situation will not improve. This woman with the issue of blood in Luke 8:43-48 spent all she had on various medical professionals, but her condition only worsened.

Time is running out the longer we wait. Have you ever been in this type of situation? Just like Abraham and Sarah? Like the woman with the issue of blood? Or you could be like the father who brought his convulsing son to Jesus in Mark 9 and said, *"Lord, I believe; help my unbelief."* There are moments when our faith is intertwined with doubt; nevertheless, this does not mean that we do not believe; rather, it indicates that doubt is being used to strengthen and develop our faith.

Faith is dynamic rather than fixed. God continually puts us in situations where we are tested, stretched, and matured in our faith. There isn't a final destination for a person of faith. But each victory through faith will equip us for the next and help us succeed. God uses every trial to strengthen our faith and prepare us for the next.

This was the situation that Abraham and Sarah found themselves in. They left their nation, their people, their family, and a location that was known to them and travelled out into a place that they did not know where they were headed (Genesis 12), in accordance with the instructions of God and by exercising faith.

In the book of Genesis 13, when Abraham and his nephew Lot could no longer live together in peace because the land could not support them both with their flock, herds, and possessions, Abraham was a man of faith, so he let Lot choose the good land while he selected what seemed to be the terrible land. However, in due time, Abraham's confidence was repaid when the country Lot had picked was full of sin and evil.

This reminded me of a friend who lost their father some time ago. Their mother instructed them to go to their bedroom and check the jewelry box that belonged to their father. And there were two rings with diamonds on them. And very instantly, the pupils of my friend's eyes dilated, and like Lot, He picked the ring that featured the large stones. And it seemed like his younger brother was OK with any decision He made. But then, as they returned to the kitchen, their mother remarked, "Jr., the papers for your ring are in one of his dresser drawers." When my friend asked his mother where his documents were, she said, "yours don't have any papers because it's an imitation."

In Genesis chapter 16, Abraham and Sarah's faith was tested once again when it seemed as if God's promise to them would never come true. In the middle of their waiting, amid Sarah's uncertainty, and the midst of Abraham and Sarah saying to themselves, "*We cannot afford to wait any longer,*" they took matters into their own hands with Sarah giving Abraham her handmaiden Hagar as a surrogate mother, which resulted in a muddled situation. Sarah's doubts and Abraham and Sarah's inability to afford to wait any longer led them to this decision.

Paul says of Abraham in verse 19, "*Without weakening in his faith, he faced the fact that his body was as good as dead.*" Having faith does not imply we disregard the facts or deny the reality we are confronting. On the contrary, having faith does not mean we dismiss the facts. Some people adhere to the fallacious religion that it won't come true if you keep quiet about something. So long as you don't own the sickness or the problem, it's not real. But that's just poor theology right there.

A crucial component in these passages that is sometimes ignored is that Abraham confronted his reality. In the end, he took responsibility for his predicament. He did not refute that he and Sarah were far beyond the age when they could have children.

Abraham was confronted with the reality that for God's promise to come true—that he would have a son named Isaac—God would have fulfilled that promise. It would be up to God to work it out. If God wanted to change his and Sarah's biological time clocks, he would have to go against the natural order of things and defy the rules of nature. The most mature expression of Christianity does not provide an evasion of reality but rather equips followers with the tools necessary to engage reality through faith.

Christianity does not provide a way out of our everyday lives; it gives us the faith to return to those lives and confront whatever challenges they bring. Having faith in God equips us with the strength to stand up to the things in our lives that want to bring us down. And it was in this way that Abraham brought honor to God. Not by denying his reality, but by confronting it and trusting that God was still able, *"Being fully convinced that what God had promised, He was also able to perform."* Being completely convinced.

Paul says Abraham did not waver. On the other hand, there were a few occasions when he wavered. When you waver, you're really doubting yourself and becoming mired in that uncertainty to the point that it prevents you from moving ahead from where you are. Abraham did not let himself get immobilized by the analysis-induced immobility that may have occurred. Is it possible that Paul is trying to imply that Abraham continued to believe despite the facts?

Abraham did not allow himself to be paralyzed by uncertainty despite the evidence. Despite the overwhelming evidence, he did not give up hope. Despite everything, he did not abandon his faith in God's promise. Abraham did not have a faith that was so strong that it prevented him from considering the truth of his circumstances.

Faith tells us to turn to God rather than the circumstance when we are put to the test of our faith, just as Abraham did. However, faith does not ignore the facts. Move forward in faith, even if doing so causes you fear and trembling, because you know that God will reward those who diligently seek Him. Even if things don't work out precisely the way you imagined they should, the fact that we trusted God rather than relying on our own knowledge demonstrates that our faith is worthy of giving praise to God.

WHY IS FAITH IMPORTANT?

Faith is important for several reasons. First, it is necessary for salvation. The Bible says that we are saved by grace through faith (Ephesians 2:8). We cannot earn our salvation by good works or religious observance.

Instead, we must trust Jesus Christ and believe He died for our sins and rose again.

Second, faith helps us to overcome fear and anxiety. When we have faith in God, we can trust that He is in control and will provide for our needs. We do not need to worry or be afraid because God is with us and will never leave us or forsake us (Hebrews 13:5).

Third, faith enables us to live a life of purpose and meaning. When we trust in God, we can follow His plan for our lives and use our gifts and talents to serve Him and others. We can have confidence that God will use us to make a difference in the world and to bring glory to His name.

HOW CAN WE DEVELOP AND MAINTAIN OUR FAITH?

Developing and maintaining our faith is an ongoing process. Here are some practical steps we can take to deepen our faith in God:

Read the Bible regularly. The Bible is God's word, and it is the primary way that He communicates with us. When we read the Bible, we can learn about God's character, His promises, and His plans for our lives. We can also see how other believers have lived out their faith in God and be encouraged by their examples.

Pray regularly. Prayer is a powerful way to connect with God and to express our gratitude, concerns, and requests to Him. When we pray, we can ask God to help us grow in our faith and guide us daily.

Attend church and participate in the Christian community. Being part of a community of believers can provide encouragement, accountability, and support as we seek to grow in our faith. We can also learn from other believers and be challenged to live out our faith practically.

Serve others. Serving others is a tangible way to demonstrate our faith in God and share His love. When we serve others, we can experience the joy and fulfillment of living out our faith in practical ways.

Trust God in all circumstances. Trusting God in difficult circumstances can be challenging, but it is essential for deepening our faith. When we face trials or adversity, we can choose to trust that God is with you always.

CHAPTER SIX

WALKING BY FAITH

Walking by faith, a lot of people have heard the word without the full understanding of what the phrase means. But what does it mean to walk by faith?

Walking by faith means that you are required to travel to a location that you are unfamiliar with, a place that God will disclose to you as you walk in obedience. Consider the life of Abraham as an example (Genesis 12:1).

Walking by faith means keeping to the dreams that God has planted in your heart, even though you have been cast away and put to jail for crimes you did not commit. Just look at all that Joseph had to go through (Genesis 37-50).

Walking by faith means taking a strong commitment to follow God's plan regardless of the challenges life presents. it requires strong determination.

Walking by faith means you have the bravery to speak up for those who are suffering, broken, and downtrodden; it also means you are willing to face death for the sake of others. Consider the story of Esther and how she put herself in danger to rescue her people, the Jews.

Sometimes acting like an idiot may be the best option. Consider the story of Noah, who prepared for the flood by constructing an ark even though it had never rained on earth before. Consider how Abraham, who was childless at the age of 100, clung to the promise that he would become the father of many countries even though he was unable to have children.

DO YOU SEE WHAT I'M SAYING

Just picture Moses standing in front of the Israelites in the desert and promising them that they would eat meat till they get tired, all the while not knowing where the meat would come from. Consider the story of Joshua as he obeyed God's command to march around the walls of Jericho while simultaneously asking what good this would accomplish.

If you decide to follow this course of action, you must be ready to go outside of your comfort zone and abandon the Americanized form of Christianity that so many of us have been exposed to for our whole lives. You must be ready to let God take your world, flip it upside down, shake it up, and start over completely if you want to have a relationship with him. For God to appear in the way he sees fit, you need to be prepared to release him from the tidy little box that you have constructed for him.

Perhaps it will be a calling to do something that you have never dreamed of doing before, such as becoming a foster parent or adopt a child, quit your job and become a missionary, or give up the comforts of this world in exchange for the treasures of heaven.

It's possible that it won't be very clean, tidy, or socially acceptable at all. Perhaps, just like it did for me, the anguish of adultery and divorce will turn your world upside down and inside out. Or maybe you are struggling with issues related to fertility or addiction. It's possible that you have a wayward child who dramatically changes the path that the rest of your life takes. Or maybe you are someone who has been through the unimaginable pain of losing a kid.

I don't know what your shake-up could look like, but I do know that if you would submit it to God, throw your arms up in surrender, and ask him to use it to modify your life, he will respect your desire. I don't know what your shake-up might look like. He will lead you on an adventure, instruct you in the way of walking by faith, and entrust you with some of the most precious moments in life.

He will plant the seed of faith in you, the kind of faith that can move mountains and the hands of God. He will show you how to live this life with abandonment, and as a result, you will have the freedom to walk in all of God's fullness and grace. He will equip you so that you might be used powerfully in this life for the glory of God.

Maybe you've already been through the experience of having your life completely turned upside down and thrown out of control. Perhaps you, like me, have found yourself lost in the wilderness, where you spend the nights watching his fire direct your every step and spend days following a cloud as your guide. Possibly, you have the impression that you are close to entering the Promised Land; all that remains is for him to issue the order for you to take possession of it.

Despite this, you feel worn out and exhausted. You have alienated some of your former friends because they cannot see how you can stubbornly hold to a promise so patently doomed to fail. You are so near, yet I feel you are so far away. You have a hard time resisting the temptation to make do with what you have, even though you are aware that it is not God's best for you. You just do not know how much longer you can hold your ground.

You are not alone. I envision God reviving a small band of faithful people, who he already knows would follow his commands. He is seeking people with clean hands and pure hearts, people who will choose obedience even if it costs them all that this world must give them. He is looking for people who choose obedience even if it costs them everything. He seeks those who will throw caution to the wind and believe that he has a plentiful life (John 10:10) waiting for us if we follow his methods. He is looking for people who will fling caution to the wind. In James 1:2, the apostle James writes that God is searching for those whose "hearts have been purified" and whose "faith has been strengthened by the trials of this life." He is seeking those who will remain steadfast in their commitment to his promises even when there may seem to be little chance of success.

God has selected you, to be a member of this remnant, which consists of people willing to let him take control of their lives and shape them into what he envisions. He has selected you to undergo a severe examination and examination of your faith, and he assures you that the fire will only cleanse you and not burn you. He has guaranteed that he will accompany you on every step of the journey, walking with you, carrying you, and supporting you. Even when life seems spinning wildly out of control, he assures you that you can still count on him to be in charge.

Ephesians 3:20-21, Now to him who is able to do immeasurably more than all we ask or imagine, according to his power that is at work within us, to him be glory in the church and in Christ Jesus throughout all generations, forever and ever! Amen.

He is training you to have faith in him so that he might perform a miracle that is greater than anything you could have ever imagined. He is instructing you to relinquish control and put your faith in him with all your heart.

Proverbs 3:5-6, Trust in the Lord with all your heart and lean not on your own understanding; in all your ways submit to him, and he will make your paths straight.

For this reason, he is instructing you to live in the spirit every single day so that he might do even bigger things in you and through you.

John 14:12, Very truly I tell you, whoever believes in me will do the works I have been doing, and they will do even greater things than these, because I am going to the Father.

He is preparing you to be a ray of light and hope in a world starving for Jesus and urgently wants to see him.

I don't know your stance on this path of walking by faith, but I urge you, implore you, and plead with you to raise the white flag of surrender. I don't know where you stand on this trip. Give your life, suffering, and loss over to God so that he can use them for his glory. For him to accomplish a great job through you, you need to ask him to do amazing work in you first.

WHAT WALKING BY FAITH IS NOT

There are a great number of individuals who do not have a clear understanding of what it means to live by faith. Let's look at what walking by faith is not.

WALKING BY FAITH IS NOT THE SAME AS BEING AN ENTERPRISING BUSINESSMAN.

Elon Musk is a businessman; he doesn't walk by faith. Does it make sense? Because of the possibility that we would be tempted to baptize our aspirations of grandeur and prosperity in this life with biblical vocabulary, I believe that it is extremely vital that we keep that contrast in mind. You probably know what I'm talking about when I say, "Steve Jobs had a lot of faith," since he launched Apple in Steve Wozniak's garage. But Steve Jobs didn't have much faith in what he was doing! He had a lot of courage, and he had an outstanding intellect, but he did not have faith–at least not in the way that is used in the Bible. Because biblical faith is attached to God's promises that have their principal fulfillment beyond this life and obeys God's instructions, these promises have their primary fulfillment beyond this life.

WALKING BY FAITH DOES NOT MEAN BEING LAZY OR FAILING TO MAKE PLANS.

Sometimes we get the feeling that Proverbs is about wisdom, but then Hebrews 11 says that we should live by faith and must balance those two notions. Obey Solomon, but not too much, for you, also need to walk by faith, but not too much, because you also want to be smart. That is not the way to think about either of these two mandates in any way! The commands that God gives are never in conflict with one another. The Bible does not contain any internal contradictions. Therefore, walking by faith does not mean going through life without making any plans; rather, it means making plans with an eye toward the bigger picture!

WALKING BY FAITH DOES NOT MEAN WALKING ACCORDING TO YOUR FEELINGS.

There are a lot of people who seek the will of God in extremely odd ways. It's kind of like how Inigo Montoya does it in The Princess Bride (if you've ever seen that movie), when he shuts his eyes, prays to his father for guidance with his sword, and then kind of fumbles about until he finds what he was searching for. You won't find God's will if you search for it in that manner. Thinking is more important than emotion when it comes to discerning the will of God for your life. Therefore, walking by faith does not mean acting on your feelings.

WAYS TO WALK BY FAITH

Before you can begin to walk by faith, you must forsake all other ways of moving forward. You must be ready to let God take your world and flip it upside down, shake it up, and start over again. The following are three ways that might help you get started on your path of faith:

SURRENDER

The concept of "surrender" has been stigmatized in today's society, which places a high value on independence. However, for a believer who is serious about walking by faith, surrender is an absolute necessity.

Galatians 2:20, I have been crucified with Christ and I no longer live, but Christ lives in me. The life I now live in the body, I live by faith in the Son of God, who loved me and gave himself for me.

To this day, I owe all I have, even my body, to Jesus Christ, the Son of God, who loved me and gave himself up for me.

When we are fixated on our own desires, aspirations, and objectives, we make no place in our life for the transformational force of God to work in us. We also deprive ourselves of the protection that God has given us against the plots of the adversary (James 4:7).

DR. SHAWN M. NICHOLSON

In Genesis 12, God told Abram to pack up and go to a new land, which he would eventually possess. But what if, rather than answering with trust, Abram had answered, *"That sounds great, God, but I have a young wife at home, and all of her family and mine would be furious if we left Haran." Beyond that, the thought of going for a long distance across the desert makes me uneasy. I am becoming older now; on my most recent birthday, I became 75 years old. If I had been younger, I might have been able to pull off an excursion like this, but this assignment seems to be too challenging, too draining, and too dangerous. I'm afraid not; I'll have to decline at this time."*

Does this fictitious reaction of Abram seem ridiculous to you? How often do we use the wisdom of the world or the hardship of our circumstances as an excuse to avoid surrendering? The harsh atmosphere of self-reliance is not conducive to the growth of faith. We, like Abram, will only be able to walk by faith if we are willing to relinquish.

REFOCUS

It's not hard to let the events of our lives take over and make us feel that our lives are nothing but a product of those events. But if we can take a step back, look at the bigger picture, and understand that this world is not our true home, then our perspective on the temporary circumstances we are experiencing here on earth may shift as a result.

2 Corinthians 4:18, So we fix our eyes not on what is seen, but on what is unseen, since what is seen is temporary, but what is unseen is eternal.

We are granted the ability to view life for what it is when we enter the world of faith. On this globe, we will certainly continue to face afflictions, but we may face them with the knowledge that we are contributing to the fulfillment of an eternal purpose. Because of our faith, we can have confidence that the same God who manages the winds and seas also controls the events that take place in our own lives. And He has a kind nature.

Exodus chapter 14 describes the moment when Moses arrives at the Red Sea with thousands of Israelites under his care and hundreds of Egyptians in close pursuit. What if, rather than acting with faith, Moses had taken one look at the furious army behind him and the vast ocean in front of him and then let what he saw decide the destiny of Israel?

The eyes we used to see might sometimes cause us to be spiritually blind. We need to readjust our priorities to walk by faith.

Isaiah 42:16, I will lead the blind by ways they have not known, along unfamiliar paths I will guide them; I will turn the darkness into light before them and make the rough places smooth. These are the things I will do; I will not forsake them.

STANDING ON GOD'S PROMISES

We can take steps of trust because the word of God gives us a firm foundation on which to build.

Ephesians 2:20, built on the foundation of the apostles and prophets, with Christ Jesus himself as the chief cornerstone.

The Bible is filled with promises meant to assist Christians in protecting and defending this valuable deposit that has been entrusted to us.

2 Timothy 1:14, Guard the good deposit that was entrusted to you— guard it with the help of the Holy Spirit who lives in us.

The more that we apply these promises to the struggles that we face on a day-to-day basis, the more that our faith will be reinforced.

Elizabeth, who is pregnant with John the Baptist, welcomes Mary in Luke 1:45 with these prophetic words: *"Blessed is she who has believed that the Lord would fulfill his promises to her!"*

Can you even begin to fathom how hard it must have been for a girl of that age to trust and acknowledge the truth of these wonderful promises? What if Mary had given in to the inevitable derision, slander, and hatred hurled at her by the unbelieving world and had declined the Holy calling to bear our Lord and Savior? But thank God, she didn't end up doing it. Instead, Mary could view her circumstances from the realm of faith and repeat God's promises to her cousin (Luke 1:46-55). This enabled Mary to have a positive outlook on her situation.

Mary understood that "no word from God will ever fail" (Luke 1:37), exactly as the angel had informed her. She relied on His word and carried out the responsibilities of her calling in accordance with it. It is not enough to just believe that the words and promises of God are genuine to walk by faith; rather, we must put our trust into action and take a stand for the Truth. If what we believe is reflected in how we live, then our faith is perfected and is credited to us as righteousness.

James 2:22, You see that his faith and his actions were working together, and his faith was made complete by what he did.

CHAPTER SEVEN

KINGDOM BUSINESS

And I will make of you a great nation, and I will bless you [with abundant increase of favors] and make your name famous *and* distinguished, and you will be a blessing [dispensing good to others] Genesis 12:2 AMPC

I started a movement I called "Kingdom Business." My tagline was "where the intersection of ministry and business meet." I understood the intersection is God. We educate and coach churches, ministries, pastors, and others so they will stay in good standings with the IRS. We show how they should be a light in darkness and how we should operate in the marketplace. We are the head and not the tail the lender not the borrower. We provide tips of how to create generational wealth that the "people" can provide for their families. Did you know in the states, the influence a CEO of a company is potentially more than Pastors of a congregation? CEO's have 8,212x more unbeliever mindshare than Pastors.

As Christians, we are called to be in the world, but not of the world. This means that we are to live our lives according to God's will and purpose, not according to the ways of the world. One area where this can be particularly challenging is in the realm of business. What type of business can we then call Kingdom Business?

A Kingdom Business is a business that operates according to the principles and values of the Kingdom of God. This means that it is not just focused on making a profit but on using its resources to make a positive impact in the world. A Kingdom Business seeks to honor God in all that it does, whether it is in the products or services it offers or in the way it treats its employees and customers.

DR. SHAWN M. NICHOLSON

A Kingdom Business serves others, prioritizing the needs of its customers and community above its desires for success or profit. This means that it is focused on meeting a real need in the community, whether it is through providing affordable housing, offering job training and education programs, or providing products or services that improve people's lives.

A Kingdom Business is also honest and ethical in all that it does. As Christians, we are called to be honest and to operate with integrity, even when it is difficult or unpopular. This means that we need to be transparent and truthful in our business dealings, and we need to be willing to make tough decisions, even if they may not be the most profitable or expedient in the short term.

In addition to being honest and ethical, a Kingdom Business measures success not just in financial terms but also in terms of social and environmental impact. This concept is known as triple-bottom-line accounting, which considers not just financial performance but also social and environmental impact. By measuring success in these broader terms, we can ensure that our business truly serves the greater good.

Finally, a Kingdom Business is intentional about using its platform to share the gospel and demonstrate God's love to others. This means that we need to be intentional about using our business as a tool for sharing the gospel and demonstrating God's love to others. We can do this through the way we treat our customers and employees, through the products and services we offer, and through our involvement in the community.

Operating a Kingdom Business requires a deep commitment to living out our faith in all areas of our lives, including our work. We need to seek God's guidance and direction in all that we do, and we need to be willing to put the needs of others above our own desires for success or profit. By doing so, we can build businesses that not only thrive financially but also make a positive impact in the world and bring glory to God.

WHAT MAKES A BUSINESS A KINGDOM BUSINESS?

Is it true that a Kingdom Business is one in which many of the staff members believe in God and in which there are daily Bible studies and prayer gatherings at noon? Maybe. But the kingdom of God encompasses more than just overtly religious pursuits and practices.

Even while there may be Christians working in or controlling businesses, this does not always mean that the company in question is a Kingdom Business. Because "religion and business do not mix," the Christians may keep their faith and their day-to-day work in separate compartments in the belief that "religion and business do not mix." The following is a list of indicators that give a holistic perspective for the Christian working in the business as well as for the company functioning as a kingdom business.

A CHRISTIAN OR CHRISTIANS WITH A LARGE OR SMALL SPHERE OF INFLUENCE

No matter how big or small, the owner or manager of a company has the unique potential to "incarnate" their value system into the company's operations. But even "low level" workers can think of this as their "parish," praying continually for the well-being of everyone in their sphere of influence.

A MISSION THAT GOES BEYOND AND GOES DEEPER THAN JUST MAKING MONEY

In a company, profits serve the same function that blood does in the body. Nobody, however, wakes up in the morning and reflects on their existence by saying, "I live for my blood." But we will cease to exist if our blood is taken away. One printing firm that I am familiar with upholds the following principles as guiding principles: to build connections based on honesty and vulnerability and to produce stunning visuals.

A PRODUCT OR SERVICE THAT FITS WITH GOD'S PLAN FOR THE WORLD

According to Genesis 2:15, Adam and Eve were tasked with the role of "priests of creation," which required them to "work it and take care of it" in their capacity as trustees and stewards. This included advancing civilization and introducing new cultures all over the planet. In other words, adjusting the kingdom of our God to fit in with the culture of the world around us. We can contribute to the flourishing of humankind as God intended in Genesis 4:19-22, by creating and providing high-quality goods and services.

THE CLIENT IS VALUED FOR WHO THEY ARE, NOT JUST FOR WHAT THEY CAN BRING IN FINANCIALLY

My friend, who works as a salesman for a real estate company, told me that he wouldn't make a deal until all three of the following criteria are satisfied: the client wants it, the customer needs it, and the customer can afford it.

THE BUSINESS SUGGESTS THE PRESENCE OF THE KINGDOM AND ENCOURAGES THE OPPORTUNITY TO WITNESS

In Matthew 5:43–48, Jesus asked his followers to consider how much more they were doing compared to the Gentiles, the tax collectors, and the heathen people of that time. Ironically, many Christians who are employed do not "get into" their jobs since their primary focus is on evangelization and the activities of their churches. There is a story that recounts how Saint Augustine received criticism for purchasing his footwear from a non-Christian sandal manufacturer at a time when there were Christian sandal producers who needed his patronage. He said, "I do too much walking to buy inferior sandals." The Kingdom Company encourages its customers to ponder the question "Why?" and "How come?"

WORKERS AND EMPLOYEES ARE PROVIDED WITH THE TOOLS NECESSARY TO REALIZE THEIR FULL POTENTIAL IN LIFE

Every encounter that an employer has with an employee is seen as a possible chance for the employee to be equipped, meaning that they may be instructed, encouraged, enhanced, and unleashed for their full potential throughout that interaction.

THE PURPOSE OF THE KINGDOM ALIGNED WITH THE CULTURE OF THE ORGANIZATION

When people walk into a store or workplace, they "get a message." Both the visible symbols and signals of culture (such as signs proclaiming that you promise excellent service) and the unseen parts of culture (such as ideals that are treasured even if they are not stated) are derived from the underlying beliefs of a culture. This unspoken culture has a significant impact not just on the employees but also on customers. Wise managers are aware that part of their leadership responsibilities includes the development of the business's culture. This includes determining which values are valued, how people are treated, how people learn within the organization, how successes and failures are handled, and whether the truth should always be revealed.

THE LEADERS ARE SERVANTS

Because the phrase "servant leadership" is so widely used, it is easy to forget that these two words do not normally go together. Even more, than they are concerned with their personal progress, servant managers and leaders are focused on getting the most out of their workers and providing them with the resources they need to succeed. The success of a leader may be gauged by the progression of his team members, as well as by the leader's ability to consistently uphold the company's mission purpose and express gratitude to all members of the team.

GRACE IS THE ENGINE THAT DRIVES THE BUSINESS

The servant of the kingdom is thrust into the "principalities and powers" of society, including its economic, social, and political institutions, as well as into competitive tendencies and unethical financial dealings when they enter the realm of business. Many times, Christians who are involved in business find themselves in predicaments in which there is no clear solution or "black and white" option to choose from. There is healing, and there is hope after forgiveness.

THE INTERSECTION OF MINISTRY AND BUSINESS

The intersection of ministry and business is a vital area of focus for Christians in the modern world. As Christians, we are called to serve others and to use our gifts and talents to bring glory to God. This includes our work in the business world, where we can make a positive impact in our communities and beyond.

The intersection of ministry and business is where the principles of the Kingdom of God intersect with the world of commerce. As Christians, we are called to be salt and light in the world and to use our gifts and talents to serve others and bring glory to God. This includes our work in the marketplace, where we can use our businesses as a platform for ministry and for sharing the love of Christ with others.

The concept of the intersection of ministry and business is rooted in the belief that God cares about every aspect of our lives, including our work. We believe that our businesses are not just a means of making money but also a platform for ministry and for sharing the love of Christ with others. By living out our faith in the marketplace, we can bring glory to God and make a positive impact in the world.

At the heart of the intersection of ministry and business is the concept of stewardship. As Christians, we believe that everything we have ultimately belongs to God, including our businesses. This means that we have a responsibility to use our resources wisely and to invest them in ways that honor Him. This includes not just financial resources but also our time, talents, and relationships.

Another important concept at the intersection of ministry and business is servant leadership. Jesus modeled this type of leadership for us, showing us that true leadership is about serving others and putting their needs ahead of our own. In the business world, this means that we need to be focused on meeting the needs of our customers and employees rather than just our desires for success or profit.

Another important concept of the intersection of ministry and business is also about impact. As Christians, we are called to be salt and light in the world, making a positive impact in our communities and beyond. This includes our work in the marketplace, where we can use our businesses as a tool for social and environmental impact. By investing in our communities and supporting local charities and nonprofits, we can make a real difference in the world.

A Kingdom Business can be a means of addressing social issues and meeting practical needs in the community. By using their business resources to support local charities and nonprofit organizations, Kingdom Business owners can make a tangible difference in the lives of those in need. This can be a powerful witness to the love of Christ and a way to demonstrate the practical outworking of our faith.

Finally, ministry and business intersect through the concept of evangelism. As Christians, we are called to share the gospel with others and to demonstrate God's love in all that we do. In the business world, this means that we must be intentional about using our businesses as a platform for sharing the love of Christ with others. This can take many forms, from sharing our faith with customers and employees to supporting mission work around the world.

In all these ways, the intersection of ministry and business is a powerful force for good in the world. By using our businesses as a platform for ministry and for making a positive impact, we can bring glory to God and advance His kingdom on earth.

PASTORING BEYOND THE FOUR WALLS

Pastoring beyond the four walls is an important concept that recognizes the need for pastors and church leaders to go beyond the walls of the church building to serve their communities and make a positive impact in the world. This approach recognizes that the church is not just a building but a living, breathing organism that is called to make a difference in the world.

DR. SHAWN M. NICHOLSON

At its core, pastoring beyond the four walls is about taking the love and message of Christ beyond the walls of the church and into the world. It is about being a visible and tangible presence in the community and actively seeking to serve and care for those around us. This can take many forms, from volunteering at local charities and nonprofits to partnering with community leaders to address social and environmental issues.

One important aspect of pastoring beyond the four walls is building relationships with people outside of the church. This means being intentional about getting to know our neighbors, coworkers, and fellow community members and finding ways to serve and care for them. By building these relationships, we can become trusted partners and allies in the community, working together to make a positive impact.

Another important aspect of pastoring beyond the four walls is recognizing the unique needs and challenges of our communities. This means being attuned to the social, economic, and environmental factors that impact the lives of those around us and finding ways to address these issues. This may involve advocating for policy changes or investing in local businesses and nonprofits to create jobs and improve the quality of life for all members of the community.

Pastoring beyond the four walls is also about being present in the lives of those we serve, both within and outside of the church. This means being available to listen, offer guidance, and support those in need, whether they are part of our congregation or not. By being present and available, we can build trust and create lasting relationships that go beyond the walls of the church.

Another important aspect of pastoring beyond the four walls is engaging in acts of social justice. This means standing up for those who are marginalized or oppressed and working to create a more just and equitable society. As Christians, we are called to be advocates for the vulnerable and to work towards a world where all people can thrive.

Pastoring beyond the four walls also means embracing technology and using it as a tool to reach people wherever they are. This includes live streaming services and events, creating digital content to share online, and using social media to connect with and engage our communities. By embracing technology, we can expand our reach and impact in ways that were once impossible.

Pastoring beyond the four walls is about being a servant leader and a catalyst for change in the world. It requires us to step out of our comfort zones, build relationships, and work towards a better world for all people. By living out the gospel message in this way, we can bring glory to God and make a lasting impact in the world.

Ultimately, pastoring beyond the four walls is about living out the gospel message in our daily lives and making a real difference in the world. As pastors and church leaders, we have a responsibility to lead by example and to be a visible and tangible presence in the communities we serve. By taking the love and message of Christ beyond the walls of the church and into the world, we can make a positive impact and bring glory to God.

DR. SHAWN M. NICHOLSON

CHAPTER EIGHT

SPEAK THE WORD ONLY

John 1:3 confirms, "All things were made by him." Him in this scripture references the Word of God as denoted in verse one. That means the Word is the substance or the essential ingredient needed to bring the things we desire into a physical being. God spoke faith-filled words when He brought the world into existence. Genesis 1:3-29 says repeatedly, "And God said...."But in verse 31 it says, "And God saw..." What did God see? He saw the manifestation of what He had spoken.

The Bible also says it is impossible for God to lie (Heb. 6:18). In other words, whatever He says will come to pass. If you don't spend time studying and meditating on the Word of God, then your faith in Him will never develop power.

In the book of Genesis, we see that God created everything by speaking. He said, "Let there be light," and there was light. He spoke the word, and everything came into existence. In the same way, as Christians, we have been given the power of speech, and we can use our words to create a better future for ourselves and those around us.

The Bible tells us that *"death and life are in the power of the tongue"* (Proverbs 18:21). Our words have the power to either bring life or death into our lives. Therefore, it is crucial that we are mindful of the words we speak. We need to speak words of life, positivity, and hope.

One of the most powerful examples of the power of words is found in the story of Jesus healing the centurion's servant in Matthew 8:5-13. The centurion came to Jesus, begging Him to heal his servant who was lying paralyzed and in great pain. Jesus agreed to go and heal the servant, but the centurion said to Jesus, *"Lord, I am not worthy that You should come under my roof. But only speak a word, and my servant will be healed" (Matthew 8:8).*

The centurion understood the power of words. He knew that Jesus didn't have to physically touch the servant to heal him. All Jesus had to do was speak the word, and the servant would be healed. And that's exactly what happened. Jesus spoke the word, and the servant was instantly healed.

This story teaches us that we don't have to physically touch someone to bring healing and restoration into their lives. We can speak the word, and the power of God will be released to bring about change.

Another example of the power of words is found in Mark 11:23.

> *Mark 11:23, Jesus said, "Truly I tell you, if anyone says to this mountain, 'Go, throw yourself into the sea,' and does not doubt in their heart but believes that what they say will happen, it will be done for them."*

Jesus was telling us that we have the power to speak to our problems and command them to leave. If we have faith and believe in the power of our words, we can speak to any obstacle in our lives and watch it be removed.

Furthermore, speaking the word of God is not just about what we say, but also about how we live our lives. We can't speak words of faith and hope and then live in fear and doubt. Our actions must align with our words.

> *James 2:17 says, "Faith by itself, if it is not accompanied by action, is dead."*

Speaking the word only is a powerful principle that we as Christians can apply in our daily lives. As we fill our hearts and minds with the word of God, speak life and positivity, boldly declare His promises, and pray for His guidance, we can experience the power of God working in and through us. Let us speak the word of God over our lives and watch as He brings about transformation and blessing.

HOW DO WE APPLY THIS PRINCIPLE OF SPEAKING THE WORD ONLY IN OUR DAILY LIVES?

First, we need to fill our hearts and minds with the word of God. The more we read and meditate on the Bible, the more we will understand the power of our words. As we speak the word of God over our lives, our circumstances will begin to align with His promises.

Secondly, we need to be mindful of the words we speak. We need to speak life and positivity, even in the midst of difficult circumstances. Instead of speaking words of defeat, we should speak words of faith and hope.

Thirdly, we need to speak the word of God boldly and confidently. We need to believe that when we speak the word, the power of God is released to bring about change. We need to declare God's promises over our lives and trust that He will fulfill them.

Finally, we need to pray and ask God to help us speak the right words. The Bible says,

> *James 3:5, "The tongue is a small part of the body, but it makes great boasts. Consider what a great forest is set on fire by a small spark."*

Our words have the power to ignite a fire, either for good or for bad. Therefore, we need to ask God to help us speak words of life, positivity, and hope.

The principle of speaking the word only is a powerful tool that we as Christians can use to bring about change in our lives and the lives of those around us. The Bible tells us that the word of God is living and active, sharper than any two-edged sword, able to pierce through bone and marrow and discern the thoughts and intentions of our hearts.

As we speak the word of God over our lives, we are releasing the power of God into our situations. We are declaring His promises and trusting that

He will fulfill them. We are aligning our thoughts and words with His truth and rejecting the lies of the enemy.

However, it's important to note that speaking the word of God is not a magic formula for getting everything we want in life. God's ways are higher than our ways, and sometimes His answer to our prayers may be different from what we expect. But as we trust in Him and speak His word over our lives, we can be confident that He is working all things together for our good.

> *Romans 8:28, And we know that in all things God works for the good of those who love him, who have been called according to his purpose.*

FIRST CONFESS WITH YOUR MOUTH

> *Romans 10:9, "If you declare with your mouth, 'Jesus is Lord,' and believe in your heart that God raised him from the dead, you will be saved."*

Confession is an essential part of our faith journey. It is a declaration of what we believe and a testimony to others. When we confess with our mouths that Jesus is Lord, we are proclaiming our faith in Him and acknowledging Him as the ruler of our lives.

This confession is not just a one-time event but a continual declaration of our faith. We need to confess Jesus as Lord daily in our lives and in our conversations with others. We need to speak the truth of God's word and proclaim His promises over our lives.

Confession is also a powerful tool in our prayer life. When we confess our sins and shortcomings to God, He forgives us and cleanses us from all unrighteousness.

> *1 John 1:9, If we confess our sins, he is faithful and just and will forgive us our sins and purify us from all unrighteousness.*

When we confess our needs and desires to Him, He hears us and answers our prayers.

Matthew 7:7-8, "Ask and it will be given to you; seek and you will find; knock and the door will be opened to you. For everyone who asks receives; the one who seeks finds; and to the one who knocks, the door will be opened.

Our confession has the power to affect our thoughts and emotions. When we speak positive and uplifting words, we can change our mindset and experience joy and peace. Conversely, when we speak negative and critical words, we can become anxious and discouraged.

In contrast, when we confess God's promises and declare His truth over our lives, we can experience His power and presence. We can overcome fear and doubt and walk in faith and confidence.

Confession is a powerful aspect of our faith journey. When we declare with our mouths that Jesus is Lord and believe in our hearts, we can be saved. We need to confess our sins, needs, and desires to God, speak positive and uplifting words, and proclaim God's promises over our lives. Let us make confession a daily practice and experience the transformation and blessing that comes from it.

WHATEVER GOD WILL DELIVER INTO YOUR HAND

We have looked at the power of the word and the potency of our confession, let's look at carrying out God's assignment. The Bible is packed with accounts of people who put their faith in God and saw him come through for them in their everyday struggles. One account of this kind may be found in the book of Judges, in which Gideon responds to a summons from God to rescue the Israelites from the tyranny of the Midianites.

Gideon was hesitant to accept this calling, but God promised to be with Gideon and deliver the Midianites into his hand.

DR. SHAWN M. NICHOLSON

Judges 6:12, When the angel of the Lord appeared to Gideon, he said, "The Lord is with you, mighty warrior."

Gideon asked God for a sign of His presence and power, and God granted his request. Through a series of miraculous events, God showed Gideon that He was with him and would give him victory over the Midianites.

Gideon and his army of three hundred men went into battle, armed only with trumpets, torches, and clay jars. They surrounded the Midianite camp and blew their trumpets, smashed their jars, and shouted, "A sword for the Lord and for Gideon!"

Judges 7:20, The three companies blew the trumpets and smashed the jars. Grasping the torches in their left hands and holding in their right hands the trumpets they were to blow, they shouted, "A sword for the Lord and for Gideon!"

God caused confusion in the Midianite camp, and they turned on each other, fleeing from the Israelites. Gideon and his army pursued them and won a great victory.

This story teaches us that when we trust in God and His promises, He will deliver our enemies into our hands. God is with us, and He is fighting for us. We just need to have faith and obey His leading.

In the New Testament, we see this same principle of trusting in God for deliverance. In the book of Acts, Peter and John were arrested for preaching the gospel. They were brought before the rulers and elders and threatened with punishment if they continued to preach in the name of Jesus.

But Peter and John responded with boldness, saying,

Acts 4:19-20, "Which is right in God's eyes: to listen to you, or to him? You be the judges! As for us, we cannot help speaking about what we have seen and heard."

They trusted in God's promises and were filled with the Holy Spirit. As a result, they were able to speak with power and authority, and many people were saved through their testimony.

Later in Acts, we see Paul and Silas imprisoned in Philippi. Instead of giving up, they prayed and sang hymns to God. God responded with an earthquake that shook the prison, opened the doors, and loosened their chains.

When the jailer saw what had happened, he was filled with fear and asked Paul and Silas what he needed to do to be saved. They shared the gospel with him, and he and his entire household were saved.

These stories remind us that when we trust in God and His promises, He can do miraculous things in our lives. He can deliver us from our enemies, heal our bodies, and provide for our needs. We just need to have faith and trust in Him.

Remember, whatever God will deliver it into your hand. When we trust in God and His promises, He can do miraculous things in our lives. He can deliver us from our enemies, heal our bodies, and provide for our needs. We just need to have faith and obey His leading. Let us trust in God's promises and believe that He is with us, fighting for us, and will deliver us into victory.

DR. SHAWN M. NICHOLSON

CHAPTER NINE

FISHERS OF MEN

I think one of the greatest signpost scriptures of all is in Matthew 4:19 – "And He said unto them, follow me and I will make you fishers of men."

To be a fisher of men, we must understand that God called, equipped, and gifted you to be a minister or an educator, a lawyer, a construction laborer, or an engineer. Or perhaps he equipped you to work in the medical field or in a large corporation as an office worker.

These professions are not your purpose or reason for your existence, they are simply the methodology that God uses in line with your natural gifting, talents, and abilities to help mold and place you where you can be the most effective in influencing the people around you.

The call to be fishers of men is a well-known phrase in Christian circles. It is a metaphor used by Jesus to describe the mission of his disciples, which is to bring people to faith in him.

The phrase "fishers of men" comes from a story in the Bible found in Matthew 4:18-22.

> *Matthew 4:18-22, As Jesus was walking beside the Sea of Galilee, he saw two brothers, Simon called Peter and his brother Andrew. They were casting a net into the lake, for they were fishermen. "Come, follow me," Jesus said, "and I will send you out to fish for people." At once they left their nets and followed him. Going on from there, he saw two other brothers, James son of Zebedee and his brother John. They were in a boat with their father Zebedee, preparing their nets. Jesus called them, and immediately they left the boat and their father and followed him.*

DR. SHAWN M. NICHOLSON

This story has profound implications for Christians today. It reveals that the call to be fishers of men is a call to follow Jesus. It is a call to leave behind our old way of life and embrace a new way of living. It is a call to make Jesus the center of our lives and to share his message with others.

Being fishers of men means that we are called to be evangelists. We are called to share the good news of Jesus Christ with others and to lead them to faith in him. This can be a daunting task for many Christians, but it is one that we must take seriously. The Apostle Paul wrote,

Romans 10:14, How, then, can they call on the one they have not believed in? And how can they believe in the one of whom they have not heard? And how can they hear without someone preaching to them?

To be fishers of men, we must first be willing to follow Jesus. We must be willing to let go of our own desires and submit to his will. This means that we must be willing to obey his commands and trust in his plan for our lives. We must also be willing to share our faith with others, even if it means facing rejection or persecution.

The task of being fishers of men can seem overwhelming, but we are not alone in this mission. Jesus promised to be with us always, even to the end of the age.

Matthew 28:20 and teaching them to obey everything I have commanded you. And surely, I am with you always, to the very end of the age."

He also promised to send us the Holy Spirit, who will guide us and give us the words to say when we share our faith with others.

John 14:26, But the Advocate, the Holy Spirit, whom the Father will send in my name, will teach you all things and will remind you of everything I have said to you.

To be effective fishers of men, we must also be intentional in our efforts. We cannot simply wait for people to come to us; we must actively seek out opportunities to share our faith with others. This may involve inviting people to church, sharing our testimony, or simply engaging in conversations about faith with those around us.

We must also be sensitive to the needs of those around us. We must be willing to listen to their concerns and offer them hope and comfort through the message of the gospel. This may involve meeting practical needs such as providing food or shelter, or simply offering a listening ear.

One of the keys to being effective fishers of men is to build relationships with those around us. We must be willing to invest time and energy into building friendships with those who do not know Jesus. This means that we must be patient and persistent in our efforts. We must be willing to show love and kindness to those who may not share our beliefs.

Being fishers of men means that we are called to be ambassadors for Christ in the world. We are called to represent him in our words and actions and to share his love with those around us. This may involve making sacrifices and facing challenges, but it is a calling that we must take seriously.

As we seek to be fishers of men, we must also remember that our goal is not just to win souls but to make disciples. Jesus commanded his disciples to go and make disciples of all nations.

Matthew 28:19, Therefore go and make disciples of all nations, baptizing them in the name of the Father and of the Son and of the Holy Spirit,

This means that we are not just called to share the gospel but to help others grow in their faith and to become mature followers of Jesus.

Making disciples involves teaching others about Jesus, helping them to understand the Bible, and encouraging them to develop a personal relationship with God. It also involves modeling the Christian life for others and walking alongside them as they grow in their faith. This can be a challenging task, but it is one that is essential if we want to see lasting change in the lives of those around us.

To be effective at making disciples, we must be intentional in our efforts. We must be willing to invest time and energy into building relationships with those around us. We must also be willing to teach and mentor others, even if it means sacrificing our own time and resources.

Making disciples also requires a deep commitment to prayer. We must pray for those who do not know Jesus and ask God to open their hearts to his message. We must also pray for those who are already believers and ask God to help them grow in their faith and to become effective witnesses for Christ.

As we seek to be fishers of men and to make disciples, we must also be aware of the challenges that we may face. We may face opposition and persecution from those who do not share our beliefs. We may also struggle with doubts and fears as we step out in faith to share the gospel with others.

In these moments, we must remember that we are not alone. Jesus promised to be with us always, and he has given us the Holy Spirit to guide and strengthen us. We must also remember that our ultimate reward is not in this life but in the life to come. As Jesus said:

Matthew 5:11-12, "Blessed are you when people insult you, persecute you and falsely say all kinds of evil against you because of me. Rejoice and be glad, because great is your reward in heaven."

In conclusion, the call to be fishers of men is a call to follow Jesus and to share his message with others. It is a call to be intentional in our efforts, to build relationships with those around us, and to make disciples. It is a challenging task, but it is one that we must take seriously if we want to see lasting change in the lives of those around us.

As we seek to be fishers of men and to make disciples, let us remember that our goal is not just to win converts but to help others grow in their faith and to become mature followers of Jesus. Let us be intentional in our efforts, committed to prayer, and willing to face the challenges that come our way. And let us trust in the promise of Jesus, who said, "Come, follow me, and I will make you fishers of men."

DO YOU SEE WHAT I'M SAYING

TYPES OF FISH

It is true we are all called to be fishers of men, but we need to understand that there are different types of fish in the river to fish for, the same way there are different types of people in the world to win over to Jesus. We need to understand that each fish has their own habitat and habits.

But as mentioned, there are many different types of people out there, each with their own unique personalities, interests, and habits. Understanding these differences can help us to better reach out to those who are lost and in need of salvation. Let's take a closer look at some of the different groups:

THE BUILDERS

There are several species of fish that are known to prefer deep, clear water lakes. These lakes are typically colder and have a higher oxygen content, which makes them ideal habitats for these fish. These fishes include lake trout, kokanee salmon, lake whitefish rainbow trout, and cisco among others.

Similarly, to human fishes that prefer deep, clear water lakes, we have humans too that can be referred to as builders. These are people born before 1946, also known as the Silent Generation. Builders tend to be traditional in their values and may be skeptical of new ideas or technologies. They may have a strong work ethic and a sense of duty to their family and community. When sharing the gospel with Builders, it can be helpful to emphasize the stability and consistency of God's love, as well as the importance of community and tradition.

THE BABY BOOMERS

Some fish species prefer fast-moving streams as their habitat. These streams are typically cooler and more oxygenated than slower-moving bodies of water and may also have a higher concentration of nutrients. The species of fish that prefer fast-moving streams include the following Brown Trout, Rainbow Trout, Brook Trout, Smallmouth Bass, Walleye etc.

Just like the fishes that like fast-moving streams, there are humans known as the Baby Boomers. These people are born between 1946 and 1964. Baby Boomers came of age during a time of great social change and tend to be idealistic and passionate about causes they believe in. They may be more open to new ideas than Builders but can also be skeptical of authority. When sharing the gospel with Baby Boomers, it can be helpful to emphasize the relevance of Christ's message to current social issues, as well as the importance of personal fulfillment and purpose.

THE GEN-XERS XENNIALS, , MILLENNIALS, AND GEN-ALPHAS

Some fish species prefer shallow backwaters as their habitat. These backwaters are typically calmer and warmer than fast-moving streams and may also have a higher concentration of vegetation and other food sources. They include Largemouth Bass, Bluegill, Catfish, Crappie, Carp etc.

Just like fishes that live in shallow backwaters, we have the Gen-Xers, Xennials, Millennials, and Gen-Alphas. These are generations of people who have come of age in different eras and may have different values and interests. Gen-Xers (born between 1965 and 1980) tend to be independent and resourceful, Xennials (born between 1977 and 1983) are a hybrid between Gen-X and Millennials, Millennials (born between 1981 and 1996) tend to be socially conscious and tech-savvy, and Gen-Alphas (born since 2010) are still developing their personalities and interests. When sharing the gospel with these groups, it can be helpful to emphasize the importance of authenticity, social justice, and the role of technology in spreading the gospel.

Each of these groups has their own unique characteristics and if we are going to win them, we need to know that habitat and their habits. Although, these are just generalizations, and every person is special in their own way. It is essential to get to know each person as a unique individual and to actively listen to their concerns and inquiries on matters of faith. Always keep in mind that our job as fishers of men is to spread the love of Jesus Christ to everyone we meet, regardless of age, the beliefs or background.

TYPES OF BAITS

Just as there are many types of bait used in fishing, there are many ways we can reach out to the lost and share the Gospel with them. Here are some types of "bait" we can use in our evangelism efforts:

PERSONAL TESTIMONY

Our personal testimony is a powerful tool in reaching out to others. Sharing our own experiences of how God has worked in our lives can be a powerful way to demonstrate the reality of God's love and grace.

SERVICE AND KINDNESS

Jesus commanded us to love our neighbors as ourselves, and showing love through acts of service and kindness can be a powerful way to reach out to those who are hurting and in need. Whether it's volunteering at a local shelter or simply helping a neighbor in need, showing the love of Christ through our actions can be a powerful witness.

PRAYER

Prayer is a powerful tool for reaching out to the lost. We can pray for those who are lost, asking God to soften their hearts and open their minds to the message of the Gospel. We can also pray for opportunities to share the Gospel with others and for the wisdom to know how to do so effectively.

SCRIPTURE

The Bible is the ultimate source of truth, and sharing Scripture with others can be a powerful way to reach out to the lost. Whether it's sharing a favorite verse or giving someone a copy of the Bible, sharing the Word of God can plant seeds of faith in the hearts of those who hear it.

RELATIONSHIPS

Building relationships with those who are lost can be a powerful way to share the Gospel with them. By building trust and showing genuine care and concern for others, we can create opportunities to share the message of God's love and salvation.

Just as different types of fish are attracted to different types of bait, different people are attracted to different types of evangelism efforts. It's important to be sensitive to the needs and preferences of those we are trying to reach and to be willing to try different approaches as needed.

Ultimately, it's not about the type of "bait" we use, but about our willingness to share the message of God's love and salvation with others and to be faithful to the call to be "fishers of men."

TYPES OF WATER

Just as there are many types of water in which fish live, there are also many types of environments in which people find themselves. Here are some types of "water" we may encounter in our evangelism efforts:

CALM WATERS

Some people may be in a place of relative calm, with no major crises or challenges in their lives. In these cases, our role may be simply to gently introduce them to the message of the Gospel and to be a supportive presence as they begin to explore their faith.

ROUGH WATERS

Others may be going through difficult times, such as illness, loss, or other challenges. In these cases, our role may be to provide comfort and support and to help them find hope and strength in the message of God's love and salvation.

DEEP WATERS

Some people may have deep questions or concerns about faith and spirituality. In these cases, our role may be to engage in thoughtful, respectful conversations, and to provide guidance and insight.

SHALLOW WATERS

Others may have only a superficial understanding of faith or may be skeptical about the message of the Gospel. In these cases, our role may be to introduce them patiently and gently to the basics of the Christian faith and to answer any questions or concerns they may have.

MURKY WATERS

Some people may have had negative experiences with religion or may be struggling with doubts or uncertainty. In these cases, our role may be to listen compassionately, to provide reassurance and support, and help them find a path forward in their faith journey.

Ultimately, just as different types of fish thrive in different types of water, different people respond to different approaches to evangelism. It's important to be sensitive to the needs and preferences of those we are trying to reach and to be willing to try different approaches as needed. It's not about the type of "water" we encounter, but about our willingness to share the message of God's love and salvation with others and to be faithful to the call to be "fishers of men."

DR. SHAWN M. NICHOLSON

CHAPTER TEN

UNDERSTANDING GOD'S TIMING

As Christians, we often hear phrases like "God's timing is perfect" or "God works in mysterious ways." These statements acknowledge the fact that God's timing is not always what we would like it to be or what we expect it to be. But what does it really mean to understand God's timing?

God is outside of time, and it is God Himself who created time. Consider Genesis 1:1, "In the beginning, God created the heavens and the earth." God is already there at the very beginning before the creation and before time itself. God's creation of the universe marks the beginning of time. So, it makes no sense to say that one day of God's time is equivalent to a thousand years of man's time. God is eternal, and any attempt to contrast His time with man's time betrays an erroneous understanding of the eternal nature of God. If there is no such thing as 'God's time', then when the Bible refers to time, it must be a reference to man's time. Thus, 2 Peter 3:8 cannot be contrasting one day of God's time to a thousand years of man's time. We should note that this verse does not say that a day **is** a thousand years. It says that a day is **as/like** a thousand years. The word 'as' tells us that this is a figure of speech, which only makes sense if the word 'day' refers to a literal day—so this is actually the opposite of what creation compromisers claim—namely, that the day in 2 Peter 3:8 is not a literal day.

Therefore, we need to acknowledge that God is in control of all things, including time. In Ecclesiastes 3:1-8, the writer tells us that there is a time for everything under the sun - a time to be born and a time to die, a time to plant and a time to uproot, a time to weep and a time to laugh, and so on. The passage emphasizes that there is a season for every activity in life and that God has appointed each of these seasons according to His perfect will.

However, this does not mean that we will always understand or appreciate the timing of God's plan. In fact, the Bible is full of stories of people who struggled with God's timing. Take Abraham, for example. God promised him that he would be the father of many nations, but it was not until he was 100 years old that he finally had a son. Or consider Joseph, who was sold into slavery by his brothers and spent years in prison before being elevated to a position of power in Egypt. Both men had to wait for years before they saw the fulfillment of God's promises in their lives.

So why does God sometimes make us wait for His timing? One reason is that it builds our faith and character. When we are forced to wait for something, we learn patience and perseverance. We learn to trust God even when we cannot see the end result.

> *James 1:2-4 says, "Consider it pure joy, my brothers and sisters, whenever you face trials of many kinds, because you know that the testing of your faith produces perseverance. Let perseverance finish its work so that you may be mature and complete, not lacking anything."*

Another reason why God sometimes makes us wait is that it allows Him to work behind the scenes in ways that we cannot see. Just because we cannot see God working does not mean that He is not working.

> *Romans 8:28, "in all things God works for the good of those who love him, who have been called according to his purpose."*

Even when we cannot see the bigger picture, we can trust that God is working all things together for our good.

It is also important to remember that God's timing is not always about us. Sometimes, God's timing is about someone else. In John 9, Jesus heals a man who was born blind. The disciples ask Jesus who sinned - the man or his parents - to cause him to be born blind. Jesus responds, *"Neither this man nor his parents sinned, but this happened so that the works of God might be displayed in him"* (John 9:3). In this case, the man's blindness was not about him or his parents - it was about God using his situation to display His power and glory.

So how can we learn to understand God's timing? First, we need to cultivate a heart of gratitude. When we are grateful for what we have, we are less likely to focus on what we do not have. We can learn to appreciate the blessings that God has given us in the present moment, even if they are not exactly what we had hoped for.

Second, we need to learn to trust God. Trusting God means surrendering our own plans and desires to Him and trusting that His plans are better than our own.

> *Proverbs 3:5-6, "Trust in the Lord with all your heart and lean on your own understanding; in all your ways submit to him, and he will make your paths straight."*

When we trust God, we can have peace and confidence in His timing, even when it does not make sense to us.

Third, we need to pray for wisdom and discernment. Sometimes, it can be difficult to discern God's will in a particular situation.

> *James 1:5, "If any of you lacks wisdom, you should ask God, who gives generously to all without finding fault, and it will be given to you."*

When we ask God for wisdom, He will guide us and show us His timing in a particular situation.

Finally, we need to remember that God's timing is always perfect. In Isaiah 55:8-9, we are reminded that God's ways are higher than our ways, and His thoughts are higher than our thoughts. We may not always understand why God does what He does or why He allows certain things to happen, but we can trust that His timing is perfect and His plans for us are good.

Understanding God's timing is not always easy. We may struggle with waiting for His timing or understanding why He does what He does. But when we trust God and have faith in His plan, we can have peace and confidence in His timing, knowing that He is working all things together for our good. Let us cultivate grateful hearts, trust in God, pray for wisdom, and remember that His timing is always perfect. May we learn to rest in His timing and trust that He will fulfill His promises in our lives in His perfect time.

WHEN WAITING ON GOD SEEMS TO BE TAKING FOREVER

Even though we all want great things in our life, we frequently demand them immediately rather than waiting. When things don't go as planned, we have the tendency to question God by asking, "When, God, when?" Rather of fixating on the "when" issue, most of us would do better to develop our faith in God. If you do not have pleasure and serenity in your life, then you do not trust in God. It is a sign that your faith in God is lacking if you experience mental fatigue on a consistent basis.

Your walk as a Christian may suffer if you have a propensity to desire to be informed about everything that is going on in the world. Knowing everything about something might make you feel uncomfortable and even do you harm at times. I spent a significant portion of my life acting impatiently, becoming upset and disheartened because there were things I did not understand.

God had to educate me to stop feeling like I needed to know everything and to stop trying to control the world around me. Finally, I was able to put my faith in the All-Knowing One and come to terms with the possibility that some of my questions may never be addressed. When we choose not to worry, we demonstrate that we have faith in God.

God desires for us to conduct our lives according to discernment, which is wisdom gained by revelation rather than head knowledge. If you are continuously attempting to figure out everything, it is impossible to practice discernment because you will be so distracted. However, if you are willing to say to God, *"God, I can't figure this out, so I'm going to rely on You to show me things that will set me free,"* then you will find that you are able to be comfortable although you do not know.

When you trust God, it is frequently necessary to acknowledge that you do not know how God will complete the tasks that need to be done or when He will do them. Although it's common to say that God is never late, in most cases, He also isn't early. Why? Because He uses the times, we are waiting to test our faith in Him to bring change and growth in our lives, He uses these waiting times.

PATIENTLY WAIT

Because the process of change can take some time, we tend to pass a significant portion of our lives doing nothing but waiting. There are a lot of people who want change, but they don't want to have to go through the process of waiting for it. But the reality is that waiting is inevitable; in other words, we are going to have to wait. The dilemma is, should we wait in the wrong way or in the right one? If we wait in the wrong manner, we will be unhappy, but if we choose to wait in the way that God wants us to wait, we may develop patience and appreciate the time that we must wait.

Patience is one of the most fundamental Christian virtues, and developing it requires work. However, as we allow God to guide us through each circumstance, we grow in our capacity for patience. According to Galatians 5:22, patience is one of the fruits of the Spirit. Because it can only be learned through experience, we cannot avoid putting ourselves in trying circumstances. But let perseverance, steadfastness, and patience have full play and perform a complete job, so that you can be people who are properly and totally formed without any faults, wanting in nothing (James 1:4).

The Bible teaches that as we grow in patience, we will eventually reach a point when we feel totally fulfilled as if we are missing nothing. Even our connection with God goes through shifts and development throughout time. In the early days of my Christian journey, I had a very different connection with God than I have today. That relationship has drastically changed. It's not quite as emotionally thrilling...but it's better.

My journey through life's many transformations has helped me become more mature, stable, and well-grounded. We get an understanding of how to trust God as we go through many different events that call for faith on our part. The more we perceive that God is trustworthy, the more we can let go of our reliance on ourselves and gradually put our confidence in God instead.

When seen in this light, it is not hard to understand how the element of time plays a crucial role in the process of coming to believe in God. If He instantaneously granted all our requests, we would never have had the opportunity to learn and grow. Timing and trust go hand in hand in many situations.

LEARN TO EMBRACE GOD'S TIMING

God instils in every one of us a desire and a dream that certain things will transpire in our lives, but He does not always make it possible for us to comprehend the specific timing of His plan. Even though it's annoying, the fact that we don't know the precise moment is frequently what keeps us participating in the program. If we knew how long it will take, there are moments when we may give up, but if we can live in hope and enjoy life while God works on our challenges, we can learn to live in trust and hope and enjoy His glory while God is working on them. We are confident in the goodness of God's plan for our lives, and we have found that when we hand up control of our life to him, we are able to find complete contentment and freedom from worry.

Joseph waited for God to fulfil the dream he had given him for many years, and his story is told in the book of Genesis. He was arrested and wrongly charged before the time arrived for him to carry out what God had revealed to him, he was supposed to accomplish. According to Exodus 13:17-18, God understood that the Israelites were not yet prepared to enter the Promised Land, so He led them on a route that was more difficult and took them a long distance to get there. There had to be an allotment of time for their training, and they had to work their way through some difficult circumstances. They squandered a lot of time worrying about the timing of God's decisions, yet God was always there to provide for them and make it clear what it was that He intended them to do.

DO YOU SEE WHAT I'M SAYING

LEARN TO TRUST GOD

Proverbs 16:9, In their hearts humans plan their course, but the Lord establishes their steps.

Proverbs 20:24, A person's steps are directed by the Lord. How then can anyone understand their own way?

Then, how is it that a man can comprehend his path? Since God leads us in ways that don't always make sense to us when He directs our paths, it's not always going to be possible for us to understand everything that's going on. If we try to rationalize everything, we will face conflict, confusion, and suffering; nevertheless, there is a more effective approach.

Proverbs 3:5-6, Trust in the Lord with all your heart and lean not on your own understanding; in all your ways submit to him, and he will make your paths straight.

If you know, recognize, and acknowledge Him in everything that you do, then He will guide you along your pathways and make them clear and straight. Although it may sound obvious, a surprising number of people still make the mistake of attempting to figure everything out on their own. Many of us have spent most of our lives attempting to take care of ourselves, but when we accept Christ as our Savior, we are obligated to learn how to trust that He will take care of us. If we are successful in this endeavor, we will be able to declare, along with the psalmist,

Psalm 31:14-15, But I trust in you, Lord I say, "You are my God." My times are in your hands; deliver me from the hands of my enemies, from those who pursue me.

There's an unpleasant revelation in store for anybody who believes they've made it on their own, for Jesus declared,

John 15:5, "I am the vine; you are the branches. If you remain in me and I in you, you will bear much fruit; apart from me you can do nothing.

A covering that pulls the help of God into our life to safeguard us is humility, which acts like a magnet. When we bring ourselves to a place of humility and say to God, "God, I don't know what to do, but I trust You," God moves to assist us in our time of need. If we don't put our trust in Him and depend on Him for everything, God won't let us succeed at anything.

> *1 Peter 5:6, Humble yourselves, therefore, under God's mighty hand, that he may lift you up in due time.*

The "due time" is God's time; it is not when we believe we are ready, but rather when God knows we are ready. The sooner we comprehend and acknowledge that reality, the sooner God may begin to act in our lives according to His plan.

CONCLUSION

"Do You See What I'm Saying? Walking by Faith" reminds us that a life lived in faith is not always easy, but it is always worth it. It calls us to trust in God even when we don't understand His ways and to have the courage to step out in obedience, even when we don't know what lies ahead. By embracing a life of faith, we can experience the peace, joy, and fulfillment that come from walking in step with our Creator.

As Christians, we are called to walk by faith, not by sight. This means that we must trust in God's promises and follow His guidance, even when the path ahead is unclear. But as we journey through life, we can take comfort in the knowledge that we are not alone. God is with us every step of the way, guiding us, sustaining us, and leading us towards a life of purpose and meaning.

"Do You See What I'm Saying? Walking by Faith" is a powerful reminder of the transformative power of faith in our lives. It encourages us to trust in God's goodness and to embrace the challenges and opportunities that come our way with a spirit of courage and perseverance. Through the pages of this book, we are invited to deepen our faith and to discover the rich blessings that come from walking by faith in our daily lives.

"Do You See What I'm Saying? Walking by Faith" encourages us to cultivate a deeper relationship with God through prayer, study of His Word, and obedience to His commands. As we draw closer to Him, we can experience the transformative power of His love in our lives and be equipped to face whatever challenges come our way.

In a world that is often characterized by fear, uncertainty, and doubt, "Do You See What I'm Saying? Walking by Faith" offers a message of hope and encouragement. It invites us to trust in God's unfailing love and to step out in faith, confident that He will guide us every step of the way. May this book inspire us to live a life of faith, anchored in the unshakable truth of

DR. SHAWN M. NICHOLSON

God's Word, and guided by His loving hand.

AFFIRMATIONS AND PRAYERS

AFFIRMATIONS:

- I am a unique and valuable individual with my own strengths and talents.
- I am constantly growing and learning, and I embrace change as an opportunity for growth.
- I am a manifestation of the divine, with a unique purpose and mission in life.
- I have the power to make positive changes in my life and in the world around me.
- I acknowledge the power dynamics at play in my relationships and work to ensure that everyone is treated with respect and dignity.
- I recognize that my authority comes with a responsibility to use it for the benefit of others.
- I understand that true power comes from within and is not dependent on external circumstances.
- I have faith that everything happens for a reason and that even challenges and obstacles are opportunities for growth and learning.
- I am supported and protected by a higher power, and I can rely on this power to carry me through difficult times.
- I am open to receiving signs and messages from the universe, and I trust that these messages are leading me towards my highest good.
- I have the courage and strength to walk by faith, even when the path is uncertain or challenging.
- Today, I am the Favor of God. Today I have everything I need. Today, I'm walking in my Victory. Today, I am Abundantly blessed. Today, I am Healed, Delivered, and Set Free.

DR. SHAWN M. NICHOLSON

PRAYERS:

- Dear God, thank you for creating me and for allowing me to be a part of this vast and beautiful world. Help me to use my life for good and to make a positive impact on those around me.
- Dear God please help me to understand my place in the world and to recognize the unique gifts and abilities that you have given me.
- God, as I navigate this life, please help me to remember that I am a part of something larger than myself. Show me the interconnectedness of all things and help me to live in harmony with the world around me.
- Dear God, please help me to understand the difference between power and authority and to use both wisely and with humility.
- Please guide me towards a deeper understanding of true power and authority and show me how to use these gifts to make a positive impact on the world.
- I ask for the wisdom and courage to use your power for the benefit of all those under your care. May you lead with compassion and empathy, and always work towards the greater good.
- I ask for the strength and resilience to assert your power in the face of adversity and to work towards creating a more just and equitable society for all. May your voice be heard, and your actions be guided by love and compassion.
- Dear Lord, please help me to trust in your plan for my life and to walk by faith, even when the path ahead is unclear.
- Please help me to have faith in your love and guidance, and to trust that everything that happens in my life is part of a greater plan. Give me the wisdom and discernment to recognize the signs and messages you send, and the courage to act on them.
- I ask for support and encouragement as I navigate my journey of faith. May we all support each other as we walk towards our highest good, and may our faith be a source of strength and inspiration for others.

DR. SHAWN M. NICHOLSON

Other Books

SOCIAL MEDIA

DR. SHAWN M. NICHOLSON

MOBILE APP

PODCAST

DR. SHAWN M. NICHOLSON

CONTACT US

DO YOU SEE WHAT I'M SAYING

PIVOT TO PASSION ACADEMY

DR. SHAWN M. NICHOLSON

Scan QR code to receive free gift

www.ingramcontent.com/pod-product-compliance
Lightning Source LLC
Chambersburg PA
CBHW042342300426
44109CB00048B/2671